SOCIAL ANXIETY

PROVEN STRATEGIES FOR OVERCOMING YOUR FEAR, CALM ANXIETY, STOP WORRYING, BUILD A DEEP SENSE OF CONFIDENCE AND SELF-ESTEEM AND REACH A MORE FULFILLING SOCIAL LIFE

JACKSON MOODY

CONTENTS

Introduction   v

1. What is Social Anxiety?   1
2. What Causes Social Anxiety?   8
3. Choosing the Right Approach   17
4. Gaining Self-Confidence   25
5. Mindfulness Strategies to Overcome Anxiety   34
6. The Balanced Mindset   47
7. Occupy the Same Emotional Space   55
8. Visualize Social Events Beforehand   63
9. Social Anxiety Disorder and Cultural Differences   68
10. Challenging Cognitive Distortions and Negative Thoughts   73
11. Diet and Exercise   78
12. Natural Remedies   84
13. The Medical Side of Social Anxiety   91

Afterword   107

Copyright © 2019 by Jackson Moody

All rights reserved.

No part of this book may be reproduced in any form or by any electronic or mechanical means, including information storage and retrieval systems, without written permission from the author, except for the use of brief quotations in a book review.

INTRODUCTION

Social anxiety is a chronic illness that can negatively affect an individual's mental health, physiology, and lifestyle. It is considered the third most common mental health illness across the globe. It can be so severe that it interferes with a person's daily life and affects over 15 million people in the United States alone. Clinicians explain social anxiety using the following acronym F.A.T.E. meaning F stands for function (the physiological aspects), A stands for Action (the person's behavior), T stands for Thinking (the way the person perceives things) and E stands for Emotion. All of these aspects are used in diagnosing and treating individuals with a social anxiety disorder. Only 36.9% of individuals living and suffering from this mental disorder seek assistance and get it treated.

Social anxiety disorder or SAD can affect a person in any age or gender; it doesn't play favorites. Often those who have gone through a traumatic incident are more likely to develop social

Introduction

anxiety, especially if they were bullied, teased, criticized or received emotional or physical abuse and maltreatment. This disorder is debilitating and causes people to avoid their families and distance themselves from friends and colleagues. More often than not, those with untreated social anxiety disorder have difficulties making close relationships and feel that their relationships are negative and not what they nor the other person desires. To someone with social anxiety disorder, they are burdening and fear that burden is too much for others, especially new people to deal with. They lower their self-worth and value and always feel inferior to other people. Their mind is flooding with negative thoughts that turn into the fears resulting in crippling anxiety and cupping with other disorders such as panic attacks and depression. Many turn to self-medicate instead of seeking professional help, which results in alcohol and drug abuse.

Doctors explain that receiving the appropriate treatment for an anxiety disorder that has been diagnosed early on and developing over a 12-month period is considered for using medications which involves at least four visits to the doctor over a few months' time. Doctors also recommend using a psychotherapeutic treatment, which involves seeing the therapist for at least 8 visits. Treating this mental illness sooner and assisting with the treatment for this disease would prevent the disorder from becoming chronic and reduce the chances of also developing additional physical or mental illnesses, such as depression.

The low percentage of individuals who receive proper treatments for anxiety disorders has a few factors that come into play. Often, many doctors and patients don't recognize that an individual has a physical ailment due to a mental disorder and so it goes unnoticed. Data shows that approximately only 41.3% of individuals living with an anxiety disorder are aware they need some sort of treatment, and that number decreases to 26.3% when that anxiety disorder isn't combined with another type of mental disorder. This, unfortunately, adds to the faults of society's health system, costs for those treatments, and the negative tones received by individuals suffering so heavily with this type of disorders, thus, even further limiting the person from receiving help and treatment. High-income countries even have difficulties with mental health treatments, only one-third of individuals with anxiety disorders actually receive treatment in their lifetime, with the United States being the exception, having treatment rates considerably higher.

Social anxiety disorder is considered a phobia and is often accompanied by another mental disorder such as depression, OCD, panic disorder or other specific types of anxieties. The best-known treatment for most anxieties is Cognitive Behavioral Therapy some medications and exposure therapy. Recent research has enhanced the knowledge on the hormone serotonin that regulates a person's mood and is a neurotransmitter that balances all functions of the brain and some parts in the body, in particular the intestines. Regulating serotonin levels has been found to help those suffering with social anxiety disorder and it is strongly suggested to live a healthy lifestyle eating high fiber foods, getting adequate rest and exercising on a regular basis to keep their serotonin levels regulated properly. Sufferers of this disease learn to detach themselves from emotions that cause anxiety or thoughts causing them to be numb and lead them

Introduction

further into depression, so it is essential for those with a severe social anxiety disorder to seek professional help. The biggest known behavior for people with social anxiety disorder is avoidance. They avoid things that cause them pain, which isn't helping them overcome their fears and live healthy full lives.

Social anxiety disorder is a serious health condition that requires treatment when it's so severe that people avoid living and interacting with people. Having some anxiety is a normal part of life that helps people adapt to how the world works and avoid dangerous or unhealthy situations. Social anxiety is purely emotion that has been induced so negatively that people have manifested it to cause fear and in some cases, panic attacks and depression. This book has brought up reasons behind the causes of social anxiety disorder, ways to help those who are struggling in particular situations with social anxiety disorder and tips to help yourself if you're also struggling with this mental health issue.

Research has come a long way since the 1970s in treating individuals with psychosocial disorders and continues to study this type of mental illnesses by analyzing individuals in specific types of social situations. This information provided gives simple examples to help explain social anxiety disorder and how it tremendously affects people with life with it. Social anxiety disorder is no longer viewed as a delusional excuse to not wanting to go out and be social and it' doesn't mean some is an intense shy introvert. It is a severe, diagnosed condition that affects millions of people in a myriad amount of ways and the best thing to do to help them is to not be judgmental, but support them and gently try to help them received treatment.

Introduction

Scientists, researchers and clinicians are confident that they can help understand even more about this mental disorder and continue to look for new ways to help sufferers find hope and relief for them, their families and their loved ones. The biggest thing that anyone living with or potentially feeling like their anxiousness is not normal, is to seek help and to get support.

Chapter 1

WHAT IS SOCIAL ANXIETY?

An individual with social anxiety will fear routine activities such as starting conversations, meeting strangers, working, speaking on the phone, or shopping. One will worry or avoid social activities that include group conversations, parties, and eating with a company if they have social anxiety. People that always worry about doing something they feel is embarrassing, such as sweating, blushing, or appearing incompetent may be exhibiting social anxiety. If you have social anxiety, you will find it challenging to accomplish things when others are watching as you may feel like you are being watched and judged all the time.

Additionally, social anxiety makes one fear criticism, shun eye contact, or show low self-esteem. Social anxiety tends to make one feel sweaty, sick, tremble, or experience a pounding heartbeat known as palpitations. Having panic attacks in which one experiences an overwhelming sense of anxiety and fear that lasts for a few minutes. Most individuals with social anxiety also have other mental health issues such as body dysmorphic disorder, depression, and generalized anxiety disorder.

In brief, one should seek help if they feel that they have social anxiety and where they feel it is having a significant impact on their life. Social anxiety is a common problem, but fortunately, they are effective interventions to reverse its effects. Like any mental health condition, most people will feel reluctant to ask for help, but most health practitioners are aware that most people are affected and will gladly help. General practitioners may start by asking one about their behaviors, feelings, and symptoms to determine more about the anxiety in the patient's social situations.

Notably, social anxiety is beyond shyness, as it is a strong fear of wanting to avoid people and other social interactions. Unlike social anxiety, shyness is a mild fear and does not significantly affect the quality of life that one lives. Most people get a mild fear before meeting new people, but once the interaction starts, most people easily cope and even enjoy the interaction. However, when we become captive to intense fear, then it becomes a phobia, and it is for this reason that social anxiety was initially called social phobia. The intense and unjustified fear exhibited in social anxiety is mainly due to worrying that people may be critical of you and that you might do something embarrassing.

With general anxiety, one worries that other people are looking at them and taking note of what one is doing. Social anxiety sufferers will dislike being introduced to other people and also find it challenging to go into restaurants or shops. If one worries about eating or drinking in public, then the person is exhibiting social anxiety. People that feel embarrassed about attending public events such as festivals, ceremonies, meetings, and sports may be exhibiting social anxiety. Expectedly, an individual with social anxiety has difficulties being assertive.

Correspondingly, people with social anxiety may hover around the venue without entering as they feel not ready to join in. Some individuals with social anxiety may think that they are claustrophobic when they are not. When a person exhibiting social anxiety manages to enter a hall where they are people, he or she tends to feel as though everyone is staring at them. Some individuals with social anxiety wrongly use alcohol to overcome anxiety, which is counterproductive.

For specific social anxiety, it affects individuals that want to be the center of attraction such as teachers, actors, musicians, and teachers. Unlike the generalized social anxiety, people with specific social anxiety can relate with other people satisfactorily. However, a person with specific social anxiety will become very anxious when asked to perform or participate in a particular activity that will trigger anxiety such as feeling suddenly weak when asked to speak or stammering when asked to speak.

Similarly, the feelings of anxiety for both types of social anxiety include getting worried a lot about embarrassing oneself in front of people as well as feeling highly anxious before getting into any social context. One will spent efforts trying to anticipate all embarrassing things that can happen when one engages in a public situation. In all the forms of anxiety, an individual lacks the willpower to speak their mind. The person will reflect continuously on the alternatives that he or she could have taken.

Relatedly, social anxiety will also manifest in physical signs and symptoms which include having a dry mouth, sweating, heart pounding, wanting to use washrooms, heartbeats that are irregular, and feelings of numbness in the fingers. Some of the other visible signs of social anxiety include stammering, blushing, trembling, and shaking. All these symptoms can be distressing and aggravate anxiety. Sometimes, one may worry a lot to the extent of exhibiting a worried look. A significant number of people affected by social anxiety tend to align their lives around their symptoms of social anxiety.

In particular, such an individual has to contend with missing out on things that they might otherwise participate in and feel contended. For instance, if one is affected by social anxiety, then he or she may not visit an orphanage, school, or go shopping. Some people may avoid taking up a promotion at work even though they merit. A significant number of people with social anxiety have challenges in building and maintaining long-term relationships. The other people with high risk for social anxiety include people with high expectations for their behavior in public and those that have stammered as a child.

Furthermore, what makes social anxiety to sustain are certain thoughts that activate when one enters a social situation and makes the person anxious. Some of these thoughts include reflecting and trying to activate the rules for oneself, beliefs about oneself, and making predictions about the future. These thoughts make one think and criticize their behavior from moment to moment. For individuals with social anxiety, such thoughts are automatic and seem to project the true inner self of the affected person. For instance, these thoughts make one imagine that they appear to other people in a specific manner, and that is usually unattractive.

Unfortunately, people with social anxiety will engage in safety behaviors that make them feel that they are in more control of the social situation. The specific behaviors include drinking alcohol, shunning eye contact, avoiding speaking about oneself, and asking many questions of the other person. The counterproductive aspect of these safety behaviors is that they deny one the opportunity to face their fears as anxiety is masked.

What is not social anxiety?

Firstly, imposter syndrome is not social anxiety. The imposter syndrome is an unjustified feeling of fear that one is not as competent as he or she appears. People with an imposter syndrome set a ridiculously high-performance bar for themselves, and when they do not attain that high mark, they feel like they are a fraud, a letdown and not worth their current position. As a way of compensating for the cost of this fear to an individual, a person with an imposter syndrome will avoid people where possible because the individual is always under the impression that people will find out that he or she is a fraud. If unmanaged, the imposter syndrome will manifest as social anxiety but as a secondary condition.

Secondly, fear is not necessarily social anxiety. For instance, if one fears that a social event will embarrass the person and that feeling is short-lived or occasional, then it does not qualify as social anxiety. There are some events and occasions that can heighten one's fear in social settings. For instance, post-trauma can manifest as social anxiety, especially where the initial traumatizing event happened within a public space. Then there are feelings of shame that can make one avoid certain places and people, but usually, this is short-lived. Social anxiety arises where the fear and uneasiness of engaging in social interactions is unjustified and chronic as well as overwhelming the affected person.

Symptoms of Social Anxiety

Those who suffer from social anxiety disorder experience major emotional distress when in situations such as the following:

- Getting to be introduced to other people
- Being criticized and teased
- Being the center of attention
- When being watched while doing an activity
- Meeting individuals who are in authority
- Most social interactions, especially when in the company of strangers
- Moving around a room and having to talk
- Friendship or romantic interpersonal relations

The psychological symptoms associated with a social anxiety disorder may include intense fear, increased heartbeat, blushing, increased sweating, dryness of the throat and mouth, and trembling among others. The most common feature, however, is a constant and intense anxiety that doesn't fade away. On the other hand, socially anxious individuals face their everyday fears.

It is important to know that only adequate and appropriate treatment works to get rid of social anxiety disorder even though very few people have any knowledge of it.

Chapter 2

WHAT CAUSES SOCIAL ANXIETY?

There are a number of different explanations as to what causes social anxiety disorder. Every person is different and every person is likely to have different triggers. Factors such as upbringing, culture, and traumatic experiences can all play a role. Here I am going to go over the most common reasons why people might suffer with social anxiety.

Behavioral

There is a theory that suggests some people develop a social anxiety disorder because of things that may have happened in the past. You know that if a child touches something hot, like an oven door for example, the pain would teach them that oven doors are something to be avoided because they get hot and they can hurt you. Similarly, social situations where you were made to feel humiliated, embarrassed or fearful could have an effect on how you feel in future social situations. You may be afraid that all situations will be like this and, as a result, you start to avoid them.

Obviously, there are a few problems with this theory. In order for behavioral psychology to work, you need to have a repetitive occurrence. This means that an embarrassing situation would need to happen to you over and over again, for you to relate all social situations with discomfort. While it certainly is possible that some people have inordinately more socially humiliating experiences than others, you would have to have bad luck for behavioral psychology to apply here.

Thinking

Another theory lends itself to the thought that some people have a style of thinking that leads to social anxiety. Someone who is anxious in social situations will predict to himself or herself that they will perform badly and they will think that everyone is watching them, judging them all the time. People who are socially anxious will doubt their own abilities to blend in and join in, believing they are boring and that nobody wants to hear what they have to say. Thinking patterns like this automatically make what could be simple nerves into something far worse.

We often call people with this thinking worrywarts or Debbie downers. These individuals rarely look on the bright side and always think about all of the things that can go wrong instead. Some people might be given to this type of thinking more than others, but often this is a learned thought process that is not natural. This is good news, though, because it means that you can retrain the way you think successfully.

Evolutionary

Evolutionary factors may also play a part in social anxiety disorder. To understand this, remember that humans are a sociable race and we tend to enjoy being in company. Some people don't like to think that they may upset other people and don't want to end up being rejected so, for some people, the start of a social anxiety disorder is a simple fact of being over sensitive to negative evaluation. This may be why many socially anxious people do everything they can to upset other people and, in the long-term they do more harm to themselves.

Biological

There is also the suggestion that social anxiety disorder may have familial ties. Look back through your family – if someone else has social anxiety issues, then there is a good chance that you may inherit their personality traits. While there is a strong correlation showing that family relations often share similar anxiety disorders, it is not known for sure whether this is due to genetics or to the fact that children grow up watching their parents exhibit the disorder, and in turn, learn it from them. However, genetic makeup may play a bigger role in social anxiety levels than we really know. Studies continue to be conducted in this area.

Traumatic or Bad Experiences

When someone experiences something bad or traumatic, extreme distress can be felt at the time it happens. But it doesn't end there because that experience can leave its mark on that person. Some of the more common of these experiences that are reported as happening to socially anxious people start in their school years. Bullying is a prime example or anything else that singles a person out to be odd, somewhat different, and unacceptable in the eyes of other people; all of these can contribute towards social anxiety throughout life.

PTSD is also a common consequence of acute traumatic experiences, which in turn can worsen an already present social anxiety disorder. Constantly reliving bad experiences through flashbacks keeps negative thoughts at the forefront of your mind and doesn't give you the chance to approach a social situation in an unbiased manner.

The Demands of Life

When you talk to people who have social anxiety disorder, most will say that they have always had it while others will say that it started when they were teenagers or in their early twenties. Teenagers and young adults have a lot of stumbling blocks to get over, especially socially, when they start to gain their independence and begin to establish their role as an adult in the roles that society expects of them.

Public schools give many opportunities for socially awkward situations and events. Overcoming these situations correctly in order not to develop SAD needs a lot of guidance and honest conversation. Getting through these challenges is not easy and the patterns that these young adults develop may have an impact on their life in the future and make some things hard to deal with. Many high school students enter college struggling with the ability to fit in and spend a lot of their time trying to impress others both physically and mentally.

Stresses of the Present

There are two types of stress that are likely to have an effect on the level of anxiety that a person feels – significant moves that server to cut contact with colleagues, friends and/or family; and significant changes that have an effect on the way a person relates to others, perhaps a change in their job at work. These demand that a person adapts to a new situation quickly and takes up a great deal of energy when, in all likelihood, there is little to spare.

Any situation that requires meeting new people and building new relationships is initially stressful, as you are trying to test the waters and get to know the other person while at the same time putting your best foot forward. The pressure to impress is great, and the fear of failure can cause significant anxiety. Confidence has to be built up and this is a time when old vulnerabilities are likely to surface.

Technology

Social anxiety disorder, which is one of many anxiety disorders, is on the rise. More and more people today seem disconnected and struggling to get along in the world. Depression has seen increasing numbers as well, and that is not the only way that anxiety disorders and depression show a correlation. 50% of those diagnosed with depression also suffer from anxiety and vice versa. Antidepressants are the second most prescribed drug in the U.S., and suicide rates are going up every year.

While we have looked at the influence of genetics, hormone imbalance, and circumstances on anxiety disorders, there is another crucial factor, which is technology. The feeling of loneliness is huge among people suffering from SAD and depression. Advances in technology given us the ability to be more connected and lonelier at the same time. But how is this possible? Let's take a look at the example of Greenland.

Greenland today has one of the highest suicide rates in the world. However, this did not start until small villages began to become desolate because everyone was moving to the capital for employment and education. You would think that people would feel less lonely and depressed when living in a large group rather than in a tiny village of only 50 citizens. However, with the increase of proximity, Greenland experienced a loss in the sense of community. A person's anxiety or depression is not solely dependent on how many people are around them. We all know that it is possible to feel the loneliest within in a group of people. As human beings we are social creatures, and without a community that supports us, we can feel a lack of purpose in life.

Technology, in a sense, has had the same effect in the U.S. that centralized jobs and education has done to Greenland. Conversation with thousands, even millions of people is available at our fingertips, but rarely do these interactions look beneath the surface and build a relationship. Sitting behind our screens we have forgotten how to interact in person, which is why so many of us feel anxiety in social situations, where other eyes are watching us rather than merely reading black text on a white background.

Technology is an excellent tool, but instead of using it as a carpenter uses a saw, we let it use us. Who has ever heard of a saw using a carpenter? Nobody. It just doesn't work that way. And yet we live our lives glued to screens and let them dictate every aspect of our lives. If you find yourself spending more time in front of a screen than interacting with other people in the real world, you may have just found one of the causes of your SAD.

If you find that you have this problem, you may need to learn how to limit your screen time. Perhaps you can set up your smartphone to stop receiving data after a certain limit, or maybe you should give it up altogether and return to a simplified cell phone until you think you can handle it better.

You may also find that the group of friends that you have is not building community at all. Perhaps you feel like you are constantly being judged because the friends you have are judgmental people. If you are constantly being nagged every time you go out with your friends, it is no wonder that you experience anxiety. Perhaps it is time to find some new friends. As mentioned already, there are plenty of support groups out there for people suffering from SAD that can become a great community for you in which you will find purpose.

In the modern era, we are quick to discount traditions and religion because they seem like old wives' tales that are scientifically outdated. However, the heritage and traditions of your culture might be more important than you think. Cicero once wrote the following: "To be ignorant of what occurred before you were born is to remain always a child. For what is the worth of human life, unless it be woven into the life of our ancestors by the records of history?" Without a compass, we are merely ships on the ocean being thrown around by whatever wave takes us. It is understandable that living in this manner creates a great amount of anxiety.

How All of These Factors Work Together

Most problems have more than one potential cause and it can be hard to separate them. However, the likely causes of a social anxiety disorder can be split into two different categories – stress and vulnerability. Vulnerability is something that is deep seated; characteristics that make a person susceptible and they can be biological or psychological – in some cases, a combination of both. Psychological factors usually come from things that the person experienced earlier in life, and biological factors are genetically determined.

Psychologically, for example, you could have had overbearing parents that were constantly expecting perfection. Each failure was a disappointment to them, so your anxiety in social situations is especially high. Biologically, for example, you may have been born with an unusually large nose that makes you self-conscious. You spend social situations thinking about whether the other people are judging you instead of actually interacting. Stress includes any demands that are being placed on a person in their current life and circumstances that may be having an effect on them at the time.

In all honesty, you cannot pinpoint one single reason why a person may suffer from a social anxiety disorder. In truth, there will be many facets to the reason and to be fair, almost every person will have a unique combination of factors present in their life. No two people grow up exactly the same way. Even twins exhibit differences. However, if you are plagued by a social anxiety disorder, it is probably less important to know what caused it than it is to know how to overcome it.

Chapter 3

CHOOSING THE RIGHT APPROACH

Overcoming social phobia may take a great commitment, time, effort and in some cases, money. To pick the right solution, you will need the right information. Traditionally social anxiety disorders are treated using medication or/and cognitive behavioral therapy. Most clinicians use anti-depressant medications as the first line of treatment of social phobia. Four major classes of drugs used in the treatment of social phobia include Selective Serotonin Reuptake Inhibitors (SSRIs) Selective Norepinephrine Reuptake Inhibitor (SNRIs), Benzodiazepines and Tricyclic Antidepressants.

Some researchers think that combining medications with psychotherapy may provide better results in case of severe anxiety disorder.

Social phobia is a treatable condition. In recent years there has been tremendous interest in the treatment of this condition. Lots of treatment approaches have been developed and people have more treatment options available today than ever before. However, finding the right doctor or therapist to treat social phobia may not be easy. Apart from CBT, other therapeutic approaches available for the treatment of social anxiety may include, Interpersonal Psychotherapy (IPT), Supportive Psychotherapy, Psychoanalysis, and Analytically Oriented Psychotherapy, and Virtual Reality Therapy.

As everyone is unique, one treatment that is effective for an individual may not suit another. There is no one-size-fits-all solution for social anxiety. Sometimes picking the right treatment can be confusing.

Self-help treatment has gained popularity in recent years. The main advantage of self-help treatment is anyone can try it and it does not require direct assistance of a doctor or therapist. In self-help approach, you're taking responsibility of your own wellness.

Everyone can benefit from self-help program and it is free of cost. If you're undergoing treatment for your anxiety, you can still try self-help program. However if you are doing well enough with medication or therapy alone, adding a second therapy at the beginning would be a waste of time. In this case, you can take sequential approach. Try one approach at a time. Start with one form of treatment and give it your best shot. Once you're done, evaluate your progress. If you find that anxiety is still there, switch to the next form of treatment.

Most treatments come with side effects. Medicines for example, they will only work as long as you take them. Quit them, the symptoms will resurface. Sometimes even psychotherapies make people uncomfortable.

The self-help program included in this book will teach the readers how to cultivate a kinder and gentler relationship with the anxious mind and body. Unlike traditional psychotherapies, this program does not encourage you to go after your fear directly. It rather focuses on mindful acceptance, self-compassion and commitment.

Conquering Social Anxiety

Social anxiety is not a medical condition, although the sufferers often mistake their condition for a medical illness. It is not a disease that should be cured. Therefore overcoming social anxiety is not like recovering from a disease. It is rather like restoring the balance and harmony, and getting your life back on track. The methods you're learning in this book don't need to be beat into the ground. Take a gentle but firm approach to them.

Set aside at least thirty minutes (this can be split up if necessary) of your day practicing the methods described in this book. Make sure to maintain regularity. This book will work for you only if you work with it.

Be patient with yourself. Changes will take time. Your symptoms did not come overnight, so they will not go away overnight. If you are sincere and stick your practice, you will start to notice positive changes within a couple of weeks.

Remember to give yourself credit for your efforts. As you work through the methods, give yourself a pat on the back as often as possible. Celebrate the small positive changes, rather than blaming yourself for not yet reaching your ultimate goal. Remember, your small improvement will ultimately lead to larger ones in time if you stick to your practice.

If you're already taking prescription medications on "as-needed" basis, try to avoid them, when you're doing the exercises. If you must take medications on daily basis, discuss with your doctor or therapist whether you can reduce or quit the medications an as-needed.

Dealing with Negative Thoughts

Automatic negative thinking is the heart of social phobia. It takes practice and persistence to change the negative thought patterns, but your effort will be paid off by significant decrease of anxiety symptoms.

Negative thoughts, perceptions, expectations and attributions make people excessively self-conscious. Individuals with social anxiety spend lots of time focusing on their thoughts, feelings and actions. While self-consciousness is sometimes a healthy sign of emotional maturity, high level of self-consciousness stops you being natural. Heightened state of self-consciousness can leave you feeling awkward and nervous. When you're self-conscious, you can't adequately focus on the people you're interacting with. As a result, you might miss important information. Your lack of attention can make others think that you're not interested in them. That will make them lose interest in you.

Learning to shift your attention from yourself to others is an effective way to deal with negative thoughts and reduce social anxiety. You always have a choice to move your focus to some aspect of the situations you are in. For instance, when you're listening to a song, you can focus and carefully listen to the lyrics. You may need to keep reminding yourself to maintain the focus. Other aspects of the song such as the music may grab your attention for a while, but you can bring your attention back on the lyrics.

Same rule is applied when you interact with someone. You can always choose to rest your attention on the other person rather than yourself.

Focus your attention on the person you're interacting with whenever you feel self-conscious. It may need some degree of practice in the beginning, but overtime you will learn to be more attentive. Shifting the attention is a good strategy for coping with mild anxiety in any social situation. Here are the techniques you have to follow:

- Remind yourself to pay attention to others when your self-consciousness makes you nervous.
- Pay your complete attention to the words and ideas of your partner.
- As you're listening, think about how the other person feels about the information they are sharing with you. Is he/she talking about something that means a lot to them? Or is he or she just giving away some routine information?
- Sometimes you will find your attention is switched to

your own feelings and you're having anxious thoughts. Just ignore the negative thoughts and move your attention back on the conversation. The anxious thoughts get stronger when you pay attention to them.
- You don't have to be worried about what you'll say next. If you are an attentive listener, you'll find that your own ideas that you'll say next are coming spontaneously.
- We can never know what others exactly think about us. Therefore thinking about how others may perceive us is a waste of time. So during a conversation, don't try to figure out what the other person thinking about you. It will only make you more nervous.

The above approach can be applied only to manage mild social anxiety. When your anxiety level is high, shifting the attention won't be easy. We will take a different approach in this case.

When we allow negative thoughts occupy our mind without interruption, we unwittingly build a prison in our own mind. Eventually we become a prisoner of our thoughts. In order to break free our inner mental prison of negativity, we have to break the negative thought patterns. There are many different ways to break the patterns of negative thinking. One of the effective ways is to notify or tell the brain that you don't want those negative thoughts. Make a statement to yourself. It will be more effective if you say it out loud. It may sound a little strange, but unless you tell your mind that you don't like those anxious thoughts, the mind will continue to support the habitual pattern of negative thinking. Making the statement out loud will help your mind realize that you're having the negative thoughts more often than usual.

Whenever you find yourself having a negative thought, say, "Stop!" and visualize a bright red stop sign or stop light. Then say to yourself, "I've just stopped a negative thought from making me feel bad. These negative thoughts can bring only pain. They never help. I choose to think positive thoughts".

You can make your own statements. But make sure to keep them simple.

If you're not good at visualizing, you can make statements like, "Wait a minute! Negative thoughts are tricking me again. These thoughts drain my energy. I won't let that happen. I choose to think positive".

Both of these methods work. Use either one you want.

The statement you make to yourself has to be rational and true, something your brain can comprehend.

If making a statement every time makes you feel uncomfortable, try whispering "Stop" whenever a negative thought arises. Over time just imagine hearing "stop" inside your head. The point is to break the pattern of unhealthy thinking by interrupting the negative thought process.

To get your mind off the negative thinking track, find an engaging activity. We can call it "distraction". A good "distraction" can be reading a book, listening to music, trying a new recipe, taking care of the garden, swimming, even doing household chores can be included in the list of distraction. As everyone has different interests and likes, it is important to choose an activity that you love, an activity that can shift your mind completely off the negative thought process.

As negative thinking is a major element of social anxiety, we have to take more than one approach to break this thought pattern and develop a positive thinking habit.

Chapter 4

GAINING SELF-CONFIDENCE

Low self-esteem typically comes with anxiety disorders and contributes to them. You might feel you're not as good as other people, or not worthy of anything positive that could come your way. The lack of confidence makes you fearful to enter new situations or engage with people, worsening anxiety, and social phobias. CBT will help you with the anxiety, but it will also do you a lot of good to build up your self-confidence.

The way we talk to ourselves contributes significantly to how we see ourselves. Cognitive distortions will bring out the critic in your head, leading you to think things like "I'm not good enough," or "I'll never get this right." To get better, you need to change your self-talk. Evaluate it carefully, looking back through your journal if you need to.

Look at how you refer to yourself and what descriptive words you use. Now consider – would you say those things to a friend of yours? If a close friend made the exact same mistake as you when you called yourself stupid, would you call them the same name? Most likely not.

It's a difficult concept sometimes, but you get to be your own best friend. If you catch yourself thinking something negative about yourself, cheer yourself up just as you would a friend. Remind yourself of all the good in you, and how much progress you've made towards getting better.

Positive affirmations are a great way to improve your self-talk. These are phrases you can keep handy to talk yourself up when necessary. Get started by writing down all of your positive qualities. Be honest, and don't worry if you sound like you're bragging sometimes. Write everything, whether it's something general like your intelligence, or the specific way you handled a certain scenario.

Out of each quality you listed, come up with a simple phrase that you can have ready to go when you need it. It's easy to be hard on ourselves, but we need to remember our good qualities and use them to boost ourselves up.

There is something to be careful of when coming up with your affirmations. Don't get too outrageous, or your brain won't believe them. It will reject them and cling on tighter to the distortion it has, convinced that you've given it proof of its truth. Having an affirmation like "I am deliriously happy every day and my life is perfect," is clearly untrue. Be more subtle, and focus on the progress you're currently making. "I am improving every day" is a much better affirmation, and it's true.

Besides being your own champion, there are things that you can do every day to gradually build up your confidence. As your anxiety improves, you'll find it easier to do more of everything. When you feel able to put yourself out there for new experiences, being more self-confident will in turn reduce your anxiety further. Read on for some easy ways to get started.

Practice Confident Body Language

A huge part of how humans communicate is body language. Typically, we unconsciously move based on our mental state. You can actually reverse this and use purposeful body language to influence your mind. A lot of socially anxious people have very telling body language – trying to take up as little space as possible, avoiding eye contact, speaking quickly and quietly, moving in ways that help them hide from the gaze of others.

You're going to purposefully adjust your body language to broadcast confidence. Not only does this come across to other people, it will also signal to your mind to behave in a way that matches your movements and posture. Confident movements actually lower cortisol in your body and increase good hormones like serotonin and dopamine.

To signal confidence, work on your posture for both sitting and standing. Keep your back straight and your shoulders back. Your chin should be parallel to the ground. If you've had poor posture, correcting it will be uncomfortable at first. Keep it up though, and it will soon feel natural. You'll probably have less aches and pains in your shoulder, neck, and back, and less headaches if you suffer from them.

Learning to remain still is a huge step in showing more confidence. Anxious people are always tense, and it comes through in the body language. They feel they need to move often and have jerky movements from the muscle tension. Start to notice these little movements you make. Simply being mindful of them can help you reduce them.

When you're standing, balance your weight between both of your legs and keep your feet about shoulder width apart. Refrain from tapping your toes or shuffling your feet. When sitting, keep yourself comfortably back in the chair rather than perched on the edge as if ready to jump up at any second. Keep your legs either apart or loosely crossed, however you're comfortable, but don't tap your feet or keep your legs tightly wrapped together.

Practice keeping your head still as well. Anxiety makes us actively seek out threats, but confident people can keep their gaze on a fixed point without worry. Fidgeting is another huge sign of anxiety. This might take a lot of work at first, but keeping your hands and fingers still will go a long way towards making you look and feel more confident.

Reduce the speed of your movements and speech. Anxiety quickens these things and it comes across to others. Walk at a slower pace with good-sized strides. Be mindful of your speech and choose your words before using them, then be sure to use a good speed rather than rushing. Add more pauses in your actions, rather than jumping from one thing to the next. Silence can also be your friend – it's okay to not be talking at every moment or breaking the quiet in some way, a thing anxious people often do.

Confident people have more open body language, while anxious ones are more closed off. Broadcast openness by exposing more of your body in subtle ways. Don't cross your arms or legs tightly. Lean back while sitting instead of scrunching forward. Imagine the difference in how you hold yourself in bitter cold and sweltering heat. Anxious body language fits well in cold weather, keeping limbs close and not moving too broadly to hold onto some warmth. Gradually move your body language into warmer territory – everything is more open and you keep your limbs farther away from your body.

Finally, work on being more direct in your body language. Maintain eye contact with people that you're interacting with. Smile often. Face the person you're communicating with and avoid looking around your environment. Think of the person you're with as a friend and ally, and let your movements towards them be open and friendly.

Break Out of Your Comfort Zone

Take some time to list the things you fear most. Organize the list and rank the items from least to most anxiety-inducing. Once you've done that, start facing the fears. Start on the easiest item for you to accomplish, and work your way up to the most difficult. When you start, you might feel like you'll never have the courage to confront your biggest fears. As you gradually work towards them, however, you'll find that you can do it.

Your fears can be absolutely anything, from calling to make a doctor's appointment to skydiving and anywhere in between. Don't take into consideration how other people might feel about the things that scare you. These are your own fears, and even if anxiety has created some that feel silly, they're very real to you.

No Mistakes, Only Learning Opportunities

A big component of anxiety is being afraid to make mistakes. That can hold us back significantly, keeping us from trying new things or taking calculated risks. Change the way that you look at mistakes. They are never failures – instead, they are learning opportunities. No matter what mistake you've made or what the outcome was, you can find something to learn from it. Because of this, you can view mistakes in a more positive light. Everyone makes mistakes, but not everyone learns from them. By seeing them as valuable lessons, you've changed mistakes into something positive.

Laugh at Yourself

A lot of people filter their humor, but socially anxious people even more so. Work on loosening up a bit. Having a sense of humor goes a long way towards making every day more positive, and making it easier to brush off mistakes and bad experiences. You might have noticed that a lot of confident people are also funny, and vice versa. They're not afraid to make jokes at their own expense and laugh at them.

This can be hard at first, especially if you've spent years beating yourself up and only noticing the bad things you've done. It can help to imagine that you're in a really cheesy sitcom – when you experience something less than desirable, think of how it would be portrayed for laughs in that sitcom. You'll soon find how fun and ridiculous all of life can actually be.

Socialize

This is, of course, the big one for socially anxious people. You'll definitely need to work through your CBT before diving into new social situations. As you're able to calm your anxiety and find yourself less distressed at the thought of interacting with others, you can start to branch out and try new things. Just like any other skill you might learn, being social takes time and practice to be good at. So you need to do exactly that – practice.

Find some ways to get out more, like social events, hobby groups, or clubs. Choose ones that really speak to your interests, so that you feel comfortable in that regard. Start going to some of these, but as tempting as it might be, don't bring a friend. Going with a friend allows you to lean on them for support, or let them carry conversations and other interactions. It's much the same as trying to learn how to ride a bike but never taking off the training wheel. If you're feeling particularly anxious, you can bring a friend to some things at first, but your goal is to go alone and meet new people.

Don't go into social interactions with a goal for their outcome. Simply be with the other people. Make small talk or chat about your hobbies, but don't hold any expectations for what may come after. If you enter every social situation with the set goal of making a friend, finding a date, or getting approval from someone, you're only placing more stress on the situation than there needs to be, and you'll be disappointed if you don't get the desired result. Instead, view every interaction as practice, and congratulate yourself for doing it. If something more comes from the conversation, great, that's an added bonus.

When you get home from a new social situation, take some time to reflect on it. Get out your journal and write about it. At the very least, write down what the event was, when you attended it, and a couple of reactions or emotions you experienced. Keep this up for a while. You don't need to record every single social outing, but try to do so with ones that you had a somewhat strong reaction to. As you improve, you can look back at the older events and see how much your thoughts on the situations have changed.

Once you've overcome some of your anxiety fears, try your hand at making your own plans. Invite your friends over for a board game night, or to go to dinner at your favorite restaurant. Ask a small group of people to go to a baseball game with you. Think of what activities and outings you enjoy, and then ask people to join you. It's intimidating at first.

Social anxiety probably stopped you from asking anyone for anything in the past. It could have come from a fear of rejection, or the sense that you'd be bothering people by doing so. However, those are false beliefs you're well on your way to overcoming. Plan your own social activities and invite whoever you'd like.

Here are some journaling prompts to answer that will help you build your self-esteem.

- List everything that you like about yourself, big and small.
- What are your strengths?
- What type of situations do you excel in?
- What good qualities do you think others notice about you?
- Think of some recent compliments that you've received.
- Make a list of things that make you happy, no matter how little.
- What gets you excited?
- What are some positive events in your life that still have an effect on you today?
- What makes you unique?
- In what ways do I give to others?
- What would my life look like if I had 100% self-confidence?
- If I had no limits, what would I do with my life?

Chapter 5
MINDFULNESS STRATEGIES TO OVERCOME ANXIETY

Mindfulness becomes much easier when you gain a deeper understanding of your own thought processes. This can be achieved by broadening your knowledge and experiences on how the mind works, in general.

Through the years, mental health experts have been able to research on and collect a vast body of knowledge about the thought patterns of socially-anxious people. In their studies, they were able to pinpoint the common reasons behind anxiety-triggered thoughts and behavior. This chapter will show you these commonalities so that you can reflect as to whether you also experience them yourself.

For instance, if you believe the other people at the party will judge you for not being financially stable or wearing nice, expensive clothes, then it is only natural for you to feel anxious.

Most of the time, however, our thoughts and beliefs about what would happen in any situation, are not based on reality. We actually tend to exaggerate them with our negative thought patterns, even though we know that nothing good will really come of it.

If you are having trouble identifying your own negative thought patterns that have been triggering your social anxiety, then you can apply the following mindfulness strategy to bring them forth. You can use either a pen and paper or a sound recorder to take note of your responses to the following self-reflective questions. After this, you can then read or listen to your answers to learn more about how your mind works during times when you feel socially anxious.

Here are the steps to follow:

Step 1: Find a quiet, secure, and comfortable place where you can spend some time alone without anyone to disturb you. Once you are there, find a nice spot where you can write or record your thoughts into words.

Step 2: Begin by thinking of a social situation that causes you to feel anxious. If you wish, you may close your eyes and visualize in your mind all the different elements of that situation, from the sights, the sounds, the smells, and the overall atmosphere.

Step 3: As you begin to feel the familiar, albeit milder, physical and emotional symptoms of anxiety as provoked by the vision, notice how you react to the situation. Become fully aware of each symptom that transpires. Do not attempt to judge or think too much about the symptoms, but simply acknowledge them. For instance, if you notice your heart beating faster, say, "my heart is beating faster right now." After acknowledging all of the symptoms, you may choose to take note of them before you move on to the next step.

Step 4: Now, ask yourself, "What is it about this social situation that scares me?" Acknowledge every single thought inside your mind in response to this question. You may say it out loud into your recorder or write it down on your sheet of paper.

Step 5: Move on to the next question, which is, "What might the other person or people in the situation be thinking about me?" Again, record your reaction.

Step 6: Ask yourself, "Is it so important for the other person or people to think of me in a positive way? Why is it so important?" Take note of your response.

Step 7: Ask yourself, "How will I behave or react in this given situation? Will I avoid it or not? Why is this my reaction?" After that, ask yourself, "What are my expectations of this social situation? Why do I think this negative thing will happen?" Record all your answers.

Step 8: Consider the situation wherein your negative expectations of the social situation would take place. Then, ask yourself, "What will I do if what I expect to happen in the social situation actually does happen? What will happen next after that?" Take note of your response to these questions as well as any other beliefs or thoughts that are aggravating your anxiety.

After doing this exercise, allow yourself some time to relax first and enjoy the things you take comfort in before you review your answers. This will refresh you and help you approach your responses in a more objective and mindful way.

Be careful not to criticize your responses or reflect on whether they are exaggerated or not as you read or listen to them. Rather, they are there simply to help you become more aware of your own thoughts and feelings, particularly those related to your social anxiety. It is also important to remember that you are much more than these anxious thoughts and feelings, and that you can always change if you so choose.

Becoming Aware of your Anxiety

Triggered Behavior Anxiety is usually followed by the desire to act upon it in order to reduce its intensity. While there are hundreds, if not thousands, of possibilities as to how you would behave in reaction to social anxiety, mental health experts have identified three common types of anxiety-triggered behaviors, which are discussed below.

Perhaps after reading through each type, you might want to also reflect on whether you can relate to one or more of them. Therefore, you will probably want to have a pen and paper ready to take note of your thoughts.

Avoidance

The most common behavioral response to social anxiety is to avoid the situation. Avoiding the social situation may give you instant relief, but it will never remove your anxiety.

Here are some common examples of avoidance:

- When the phone is ringing and you muffle it with a pillow or put it on silent mode after it stops
- When you turn down offers to do an interview or present a report
- When you make up excuses to avoid attending a social event
- When you purposefully choose a different, albeit less convenient, route to a destination to avoid a certain person or group of people

Have you ever avoided certain social situations before due to your anxiety? Browse through your notes (especially the ones from and think of other situations that you have avoided in the past as well as your reasons for doing so.

Constant Reassurance Seeking

A strong desire to appear in a certain way to other people is common among many of those with social anxiety. Therefore, they constantly seek reassurance to ensure that they still have these qualities.

Some examples of constant reassurance seeking are described below:

- When you ask your friend or partner if you are fat, unattractive, and so on
- When you constantly check the mirror to make sure that your hair, outfit, clothes, etc., are perfect

- When you post too many pictures of yourself online and then check if anyone approves of them (such as how many "likes" it gets on Facebook, etc.)

While there is nothing wrong with seeking reassurance every now and then, the confidence of socially-anxious people in a given situation relies too much on it. The problem lies in their belief that something is wrong with them if they do not have such qualities. It also negatively supports anxiety-provoking thoughts such as worrying about how other people see them or think about them.

Moreover, their peers and family might grow exhausted from having to reassure them constantly, especially since they are being compelled to make judgments.

It can be difficult to detect whether you seek constant reassurance, especially if you have been unaware of it. However, you can start to become more mindful of your thought patterns so that you can watch for any signs of this defense mechanism for social anxiety. You can also reflect on certain situations wherein you resorted to this tactic and then try to consider your underlying reasons for doing so.

Overcompensation

When a person with social anxiety believes he or she has certain flaws, he or she would find a way to overcompensate in order to hide them, even though most of the time these flaws are purely perceived by their imagination.

Take a look at the following situational examples of overcompensation:

- Over-preparing for a report or presentation, such as by memorizing word-for-word even though it is not necessary
- Rehearsing what to ask and how to respond to a future conversation with a date or friend
- Trying so hard to be entertaining, charming, etc., even though you feel uncomfortable and unnatural doing so because you fear people would think you are boring
- Putting on too much makeup, wearing flashy clothes, etc., to hide a physical feature you are insecure about

Just like the constant reassurance seeking defense mechanism, overcompensation can be hard to detect especially if you have convinced yourself that such behavior is simply a part of your identity. However, by paying attention to how you really feel and what you truly think about these behaviors, you can overcome your insecurities and become truly confident in yourself.

Now that you have a better understanding of how your mind works, the next step is for you to create a series of steps towards mindfully responding–rather than merely reacting– to your social anxiety.

While no one can truly predict or control the kinds of thoughts that pop up in our heads, we do have the power to question them and interpret them. By interpreting your anxious thoughts in a curious, compassionate, and open way, you can reprogram your flight or fight response towards a given social situation.

Mindfulness Techniques to Enhance Self-Esteem in Social Situations

We all experience having low self-esteem every now and then, but in people with social anxiety, it is experienced almost every day. It becomes especially low during moments when they are about to face the social situation which they fear the most.

It can be comforting to simply avoid these social situations, but the healing process only starts when one mindfully reflects on the underlying cause. Why do these social situations cause you anxiety? How can you regain your self-esteem now that you know of these triggers?

You alone will be able to answer these questions. To help you discover them, you can use the following mindfulness techniques as your guide: Become Mindful of your Reactions Mindfulness is about enjoying the present moment in an open, non-judgmental way. However, mindfulness can also be interpreted as remembering things in a compassionate and curious way. Looking into how you reacted to given social situations in the past can help you find out why they caused you to feel stressed and scared. Then, you can use these discoveries to help you regain self-esteem and overcome your social anxiety bit by bit.

Here are the steps to do this:

Step 1: Find a quiet, comfortable place where you can sit and write down your thoughts for a while. Bring a pen and paper with you.

Step 2: As you sit with pen and paper in hand, close your eyes and focus on your breath for a few minutes. Let your mind be filled with nothing but thoughts of the sensations you feel as you breathe.

Step 3: When you are ready, try to call to memory a time when you felt unconfident during a social situation. Allow your mind to picture out the details as vividly as you can, including your reaction to the situation. After that, slowly open your eyes and write down the details on the sheet of paper. Here is an example: Last Monday, my old high school classmate invited me to a lunch gathering with our other classmates. At first, I could not say no, but I was able to find an excuse and so I told her that I could not make it. I was so relieved afterwards.

Step 4: Describe the sensations and emotions you felt for not being confident in that social situation. Try to recall the thoughts that crossed your mind during that time. Then, write down everything you can remember.

For example: I pretended to smile when she told me to attend the gathering. However, deep inside I was already thinking about how nice she still looks while I'm starting to get heavy around the edges. I had seen on Facebook how amazing her little family is and how they always travel during the summers. It makes me feel bad and I worry that my other classmates might ask me about my life during the gathering. I remember my heart racing and my head pounding at the thought... so, I had to say no.

After this short exercise, give yourself some time to breathe and relax before you read through your notes. Be mindful, compassionate, and non-judgmental towards yourself as you read, because what you wrote is raw and honest, and serves as groundwork for your progress.

Recognize and Let Go of Assumptions

Incorrect assumptions can eat away your self-esteem quickly unless you catch them as they come to mind. However, it is difficult to step out of your assumptions once they are there, so the better way is to equip yourself with the knowledge and mindfulness to prevent them or counteract them in a healthy way. Socially-anxious people make five main types of assumptions, namely Overestimation, Personalization, Catastrophizing, Mind Reading, and Black and White Mentality. Read through each type and then reflect on whether your anxious thoughts fall under any of them.

Overestimation is when you make an assumption that something is highly likely to happen, or that what you think the other person is thinking is most likely true.

For instance, someone who is scared of meeting new people might assume that in the next acquaintance party he or she is going to make a bad impression. Another example is when a socially-anxious person who does not think he or she is attractive enough would assume that the people at the party would find him or her to be unattractive.

Here are example statements of Overestimation:

- Now that my partner has left me, I am certainly going to die alone and depressed.
- My family thinks I am a disappointment.

- My friend only feels sorry for me because I could not find a good job.

Personalization

This type of assumption is when you take a negative situation personally, in that you believe it to be your fault when in fact, there are plenty of other factors that contribute to it.

For instance, if you see some people fall asleep during your speech, you would immediately assume that you are not a good speaker. However, it is also possible that the topic was just not something the audience could relate to, or that it was the time of the day when people are generally sleepy, or that there are still people who are listening intently to you. Unless you become mindful that you are personalizing the incident, you could end up avoiding similar social situations in the future.

Here are examples of Personalization statements:

- After talking for only a few minutes, my new co-worker excused herself from the conversation. I guess that makes me a pretty boring conversationalist.
- My seatmate looks agitated. She must be really mad at me for sitting next to her.
- That guy across the room is staring at me. He must be disgusted by my outfit right now.

Catastrophizing

This is the assumption that something terrible is about to

happen to a social situation. While we all do experience unfortunate incidents in social situations from time to time, such as embarrassing ourselves in front of others or committing some sort of social faux pas, some of us can just shrug it off and not keep the memory of it from allowing us to have a good time with others.

In many socially-anxious people, however, this thought is often generalized, so much so that they think it will happen in all future social situations.

Here are some example statements of Catastrophizing:

- It would be a catastrophe if I sing off-key on stage.
- I cannot imagine how terrible it would be if they see how bad my skin is at the reunion.
- I will only make a fool of myself if I volunteer, I am sure of it!

Black and White Mentality

This type of assumption is when a person judges anything as either perfect or unacceptable. A socially-anxious person would consider him or herself to either be perfect or face the consequences of rejection. It is for this reason that many perfectionists avoid social situations in which they might be judged for their "flaws."

In addition, socially-anxious people tend to use should statements most of the time, such as should, must, ought to, always, and never. For instance, they would say, "I should never make any mistakes," "I must never be laughed at, or else I will become the unwitting class clown," "I ought to look perfect whenever my ex sees me, or else!" or "I never bother the teacher with my stupid questions." All these lead to unrealistic expectations for themselves and others.

Chapter 6

THE BALANCED MINDSET

We hear the term 'mindset' used in a number of places these days. It has become quite popular in the new age vernacular. And it's about time too, because we need to grapple with it and understand this framework that we call a mindset. It is especially relevant when we talk about social anxiety because anxiety - be it social, general or specific, cannot exist (save for physiologically-caused anxiety) when the mindset is such that it is not allowed to fester. How we keep our mindset and how we thrive on it is a major determinant of the quality of life we enjoy.

Mindset

What is the mindset? In technical, psychological, neuroscientific terminology mindset refers to the conceptual state of mind. We all have a general mindset and we also have transient mindsets. In most cases, our general mindset overrules our transient mindset, but that is not a guaranteed outcome, and it is not always the case. Certain triggers can cause a different mindset to emerge in dominance and take control. For those who are well versed with social anxiety, you know that when you are faced with certain conditions, your mindset instantly shifts from one to something completely different.

We all have this metamorphosis from Dr. Jekyll to Mr. Hyde and we all grapple with it in different ways. Some have anger issues, triggered under certain conditions. Or it may be sadness and depression, triggered by a certain set of events, or we may have some form of a phobia, compulsiveness, obsession or action triggered by some form of anxiety. Some people tend to stress-eat. Smokers, whip out their cigarettes and light up, and the list goes on. There is a corresponding mindset for each of our specific triggers.

But what is a mindset?

There are many definitions of it and this book shall not take a purely academic approach to trying to relate the concept of mindset but instead we will try to relate it to you so that you may use your own life's experiences to intimate what mindsets are and what your triggers are for a different mindset.

It will also be worthwhile to keep yourself well-versed with the various hazards of the fear circuitry as we talked about in the section on fear.

A mindset is not something that you can see on a brain scan. There is no physical representation of mindset that the brain can

Social Anxiety

visually display. Think of it in this way. You can see your smartphone. You can use it to make calls, you can use it to capture images and send emails. You can see the chips and boards and drives inside if you dared to pop it open, but you could not see the algorithm that made all these things happen. You could deduce them if you observed the features of the device and its performance.

Mindsets are like those algorithms that run the moment certain events are triggered. In one moment your smartphone is a phone, the next moment it's a camera - totally different behavior and skill set.

Mindsets do that to you as well. One moment you can be totally empathetic and then there is a trigger and you suddenly become totally selfish. This is normal, your not crazy and even the classic story of Jekyll and Hyde was telling us what it is like to struggle between two sides of our self in different situations.

Social anxiety is the same way. I have seen really confident people reduced to shreds the moment they are in front of strangers. How could they be confident, yet socially anxious at the same time? The answer, it turns out, is that the algorithm that runs their state - their mindset, gets switched based on the trigger.

You are the same way as well. Even if you have a clinical issue where you have an overactive amygdala, the amygdala controlled mindset does not kick in until you are presented with certain triggering events. Knowing this gives you two opportunities to counter your social anxiety. The first opportunity is to trace the series of events that end in anxiety symptoms. The second is the series of events that calm those feelings. If you can trace each event of anxiety and tie it back to the triggers that cause it and the events that calm it, you will be able to get a profile of your own mindset that relates to the social anxiety that you experience.

Balanced Mindset

Now it is time that you understand the concept of a balanced mindset. It's not that difficult and the way you go about achieving it really is easy to do. It just needs a little discipline and faith on your part.

What is a balanced mindset?

A balanced mindset is one where you tell yourself that you are searching for balance in all things. Whether it is weight perception, intelligence perception, wealth perception. Whatever metric you see yourself with is one that is going to be tempered by balance. Take for instance wealth. If you see yourself as someone who is destined to be super rich and that everything that you do is designed to get you to the point that you are the richest person in the world, then you need to change that and think in terms of the balance of wealth. Even the current wealthiest person in the world did not start out wanting to be the wealthiest man in the world. Neither did the last one. The focus was on achieving something - the rewards came later. So, if you look at wealth in balance, you will find that not everything is do-or-die.

The core of social anxiety is the feeling that you will be judged harshly or that you will not live up to someone's expectations. Think about that carefully. It is not the person's expectations that you are weighing. Of course not. How can it be? You don't know what they are. If you know what those expectations were you would just get up and satisfy them. But you don't know what those expectations are and you place undue stress on yourself to conform to something that you do not know. It is about the fear of the unknown and the fear of becoming obscure in the face of the audience. But you don't know what they are thinking and you have juxtaposed what you are thinking onto what you think they are thinking. So what you have to do is balance your mindset by looking at what is rationally and logically true.

The core of social anxiety is the mindset that the person who you are presenting to or meeting will think poorly of you. So let's break that down.

The first thing is that you are looking for approval. Don't. You do not need anyone's approval for anything. There is nothing anyone can say or do that should affect the way you think about yourself. Working for someone else is a different matter. There you are placed to do what they want and so you do things according to what they want and if you can do that there is no issue. But in a social setting, there is nothing that they can compel you to do or judge you for how you do things.

The second thing is that you think that the person is not going to approve and they have a poor opinion of you. How do you know that? You don't. So worrying about something that you are not sure about is a pure waste of resources. However, that is typically not the case, but instead, it could be that you are a perfectionist and that you yourself do not think that the job is good enough, so that brings us to the third element.

Do the necessary background work to the point that you know what you are talking about, backward and forward. Sometimes anxiety is a subconscious message that is trying to tell you that you need to be more prepared. Keep yourself prepared at all times and do what you are doing well and you have nothing more to be afraid of.

If you have nothing to say, don't say anything. People respect silence more than they do a person who blabbers. So if you have nothing to say, then staying quiet and giving yourself that option will alleviate any pressure you may feel to speak.

Finally, moderate your expectations and know that if you miss this bus, there is always another one. Do not place such high expectations on yourself that each meeting, each presentation, and each encounter must be one that has a super outcome.

If you can have this balanced mindset then you will go a long way in depressurizing your own mind and not having so much expectation of what you should accomplish.

Social Animals

Have you heard the saying that human beings are social animals? It is indeed true that human beings get a lot accomplished because we are reliant on the social aspect of the human equation. There is a tremendous amount of benefit that we gain from the social interaction and you can see how important social interaction is by how popular the internet has become the moment social tools became a part of the internet - think Facebook, Twitter and so on.

The human psyche is dependent on a network of interactions and that has a huge bearing on how we anticipate each meeting. However, the thing that you want to understand is that while it is for our survival to make connections and to link-up, hook-up and meet-up, the law of averages tells us that its OK if not every single meeting goes awesomely. You don't have to make every encounter one that people think that you are the greatest thing since sliced bread. You will survive and your fear of abandonment or social acceptance is unfounded if you think that each and every encounter must be solid.

Making Connections is Natural

This brings us back to one topic that needs to also be understood and that is how you see yourself. Making connections is natural - whether those connections are good or bad is a different matter entirely.

When a person who has social anxiety typically gets nervous and anxious when they think of what others think of them, the sticking point is that they are worried about one of two things. The first is that they are worried that the other side doesn't see them as they see themselves. This means one of two things. One that they see themselves very highly but do not have the confidence that the other person will see what they see. The second is that they see themselves very lowly and are afraid that's what the other person is going to see.

So it comes back to you. How do you see yourself? What is your view of yourself and what is your mindset about that perspective?

To be able to cope with social anxiety you need to do two more things in addition to all the other things that we have talked about in this book. You need to change the expectations you have of yourself. The second is that you have to learn to forgive yourself for not living up to your ambitions or expectations. That is the nature of expectations, they are meant to propel us higher so, by definition, you will never be at the level of your expectations because when you reach it, you have to set higher goals and instantly you are not living up to it again. But that' exactly what you need. Understand that, and understand that you are worth more than what one person (or a group) can measure you in one meeting.

Chapter 7

OCCUPY THE SAME EMOTIONAL SPACE

In this chapter, we are going to talk about emotional conversations.

Believe it or not, the vast majority of signals you send to somebody in the course of the conversation does not involve the words you say. I know, that sounds crazy because usually, people think about the words leaving their mouths. Well, that's actually the most conscious part of communication. There's a lot of value in that, but you need to go beyond the obvious.

You're actually saying a lot of non-verbal signals. By being mindful of non-verbal signals, you become a better communicator. Here's what you need to do.

Look people in the eye

I don't know about you, but the last time I talked to somebody who didn't look me in the eye, I felt insulted. I felt that this person was trying to hide something. This person showed disrespect because if you truly consider the person in front of you worthy of talking, you would look them in the eye. Of course, you have to do this with smiling eyes.

You can't look at them the same way Manny Pacquaio looked at Floyd Mayweather during their prized fight face-off. You know, you lift your chin up and look at them down your nose. That is not the kind of eye contact I'm talking about.

Look people in the eye with smiling eyes. This shows them in no uncertain terms that they are important, they matter, and this conversation is important to you. You are not blowing them off. This is not an afterthought. This is not a conversation that you're forced to have. This is real to you. It's that important.

Emote with your eyes

I see this a lot with my wife. When she talks to people, she's not just saying things with her words. You can easily tell what she means when you like in her eyes because she has this amazing emotional vocabulary. It's not just with the positioning of her eyes, but the muscle around her eyes. You can tell exactly whether she's upset, frustrated, happy, expectant, hopeful, inspired, and it's all in her eyes.

You can do it too. The thing here is to be conscious of all the signals you are sending with your face because facial expression goes a long way. You can say the kindest, most uplifting and most gratifying words in history, but if your face looks like you're in the middle of a funeral, it's really not going to go over well.

Emote with your tone of voice

How you say something is just as important as what you have to say. When you emote with your tone of voice, you say so many things. You position the text of your speech. You set context and expectations. You also set limits. Your tone of voice is very important. Be mindful of it.

I know you're reading this, so it seems like I'm speaking in one tone, but you need to get past that. You need to imagine yourself speaking to a person and be aware of the contrasts between the words in printed form and the words as received by a person's ears. These are two totally different things.

This also highlights why you should be very careful about how to send emails. Emails do not have tones. You may have all the love, compassion and care in your heart when you type something out, but all bets are off when it reaches the other end because there is no tone. This is why emojis were invented.

Emote with the tone of your voice. Use it as a tool and be mindful of it. You must use it to emphasize and give shape to whatever it is you're saying.

Remember: This is not a competition nor it is combat

When you're in the same emotional space, it's very easy to feel touchy. It's very easy to feel like you're on the spot and you have to defend yourself. Welcome to the club! This is human nature, but you need to override this.

Understand that when you're engaged in a conversation, you're trying to make people comfortable around you. Now, there are certain discussions where it makes perfect sense for you to be combative. But if you're trying to meet somebody new or you're trying to get a deal going, you need to make people comfortable.

How do you make this happen? Well, you can do this by first allowing yourself to be comfortable. Again, we're talking about the emotional space. You have to remember that people read you emotionally. They're not just reading you textually based on the words you say. They don't just pay attention to these signals you're sending through your body language. They are also reading you emotionally.

You can consider this the Sixth sense. Some people are better at it than others. Psychologists call it emotional intelligence. Regardless of how you label it or how aware you are of it, you need to understand that this is a thing. This is real. And oftentimes, the best way to make people comfortable around you emotionally is to be comfortable yourself.

The more comfortable they are, the more comfortable they feel. The more comfortable they get, the more comfortable you feel. This goes on and on. You reinforce each other's comfort level.

Now, please understand that this works in the opposite direction as well. If you're uncomfortable, sooner or later, people around you will feel uncomfortable. Once you detect that they're not really having that good of a time, you feel even more upset, discouraged, diminished, stressed out, or anxious. You then send out signals, and this leads to a downward spiral. Down and down it goes.

The good news is that it's your choice. When you get in there, you set the tone. Be comfortable. How do you do this? Well, always remember what you're not trying to achieve. You're not trying to be right. You're not trying to win a debate. You're not trying to interrogate. Understand this. These do not have any place in your mission.

Again, in certain conversations, this makes a lot of sense. For example, if you're supervising and you caught somebody stealing, you're going to have to engage in these types of conversations but not now. You're trying to meet a member of the opposite sex. You're on your second date and you're trying to know each other more. You may be in a job interview or in a business networking meeting. The name of the game is a comfort.

It's okay to overreact at certain times

Believe it or not, there are certain times in a conversation where it makes a lot of sense to overreact. By overreacting, I'm talking about exaggerated emotional responses. Again, don't go overboard because there is a line that you can cross where your overreaction comes off as mockery. You're basically making the person feel stupid. You're rejecting the person. You're making them feel that somehow or someway, they are inferior. That's not the kind of impression you should be trying to create.

You're trying to get to feel that they matter, they are accepted, and they can get comfortable with you. So understand this background when choosing to overreact. It's okay to do that, but there are limits.

So when is it okay to overreact? Well, when people are telling a story, it's probably a good time. When you overreact, you're basically telling them, "Whoah! I'm with you." or "Wow! That's really amazing." You're basically complimenting them. You must do this sincerely and authentically. You're not just faking it until you make it.

Also, when people are trying to get you in on a joke. Now, this is not kind of like a public joke, where it's obvious that they're joking. Instead, they have an internal joke, and they're trying to figure out in their mind whether you can get it or not. In other words, are you one of them?

This is one of the most powerful ways to build rapport because a lot of powerful people operate at this level. They say, "Is this guy or this woman one of us?" Let's test this person. Can they get the inside joke?

Sometimes, the joke takes the form of a look, with a smile on their face. When you bounce it back to them, they would instantly know that you're on the same mental wavelength. All of a sudden, you're a friend. You're no longer this stranger.

Regardless if you are overreacting to a story or a joke, understand that you should not overdo it. I cannot repeat this enough because if you overdo it, you come off like you're mocking the person. I remember one time when somebody cracked a joke. It was a pretty mild joke, but I blew up laughing.

Instead of the person appreciating that I was laughing, he took it as an insult. Basically, he thought that I was making fun of him for making such an ill-timed joke.

So, instead of building a wall and mutual comfort, it built a great wall before us. The person was thinking, "This person is always judging me. This person is thinking he is so superior to me. Forget this person."

Do you see where I am coming from here? I did not have any malice. I actually really liked the joke but I forgot that threshold. Don't go over that threshold. You don't want to come off as mocking. Instead of a being a friend, the relationship gets frozen and you just remain strangers to each other.

The power of inside references

After you have been talking to someone for a while, remember what they said early on and try to refer to it. This is a very powerful conversational tool because this puts them on notice that you understand them. This puts them on notice that you are truly paying attention and that you have taken this to a personal level. This is not just something that you listen to with one ear and out it goes out the other ear.

They feel that "Wow! This person really gets me." Now, here is the trick. You can't do this with a trivial issue. For example, I remember going out on a date with this very amazing woman. I mean she was a Washington lawyer, really well-paid, really good-looking, I'm talking about model quality. She lived in the East Coast.

Things were going well as we were walking up a hill in San Francisco. Then, she was telling me that when she was a kid, the most comforting memories she had was that she actually lived in a room in her parents' home, where there were a washer and dryer. At first, she wasn't really all that happy because a washer and dryer obviously can be quite noisy. But eventually, she would always look forward to that comforting, rocking motion with the dryer and its color blue.

As the conversation went on, I then referred back to the color of the dryer. Basically, I put her on notice that with all these things that you're talking about, you just focused on the color of the dryer instead of the fact that you had this really personal piece of info that you shared with me about being comforted by the rocking motion of the dryer.

It doesn't really matter what color it is. So it kind of cheapened things. It kind of dialed back the intimacy that we were building and the conversation was not as good from that point on.

So please understand that inside references are a double-edged sword. They can work for you really well, but if you botch them up, you can freeze the conversation. You can't focus on a trivial issue when you do this. If you pull this off properly, inside references make you more likable. You'll basically reach a point where a person would say, "You know something about me that other people don't because you made the effort. I like you because of that." So do you see how this works?

Chapter 8

VISUALIZE SOCIAL EVENTS BEFOREHAND

Visualizing is a much-underutilized method for improving social skills. This hack is practiced by many successful people, and it has helped them be the best version of themselves and attract their desires.

At the heart of visualization is the ability to utilize your imaginative side. In this way, you can visualize your desired result. It could be a game an event or any activity. For instance, if you are facing challenges at your university and there's a likelihood that you'll drop, using visualizing you may get to watch yourself accepting your college degree. Well, it puts the mind in gear to do everything possible to reach this goal of getting a degree.

Some of the benefits of visualization include:

- Boosting your motivation to take the essential actions to attain your dreams

- Increases your likelihood of attracting important people who are going to be critical to your success
- Improves your brain's capacity to perceive things
- Develops your subconscious mind

Important things to remember about visualizing:

<u>Set the right environment</u>: visualizing is most fruitful when done in an enabling environment. What makes a good environment? Peace and tranquility. You can never gather enough mental force to visualize something if you are surrounded by loud annoying people and/or events. Not only should the external environment be great for you but also the internal environment as well i.e. the mind.

<u>Have the right outlook</u>: which means, the event that you are trying to visualize should be within reason. If your hopes are unreasonable then you might very well be wasting your time. For instance, if you are an overweight jobless person in the Sahara, you have no business visualizing marrying an infamous model in New York City, it's possible but very far away and improbable.

<u>Bring the inspiration</u>: these are the materials that will help you call up the image of the event or activity that you want to visualize. Some of us have powerful enough minds that we won't even require additional inspiration. But others might need to have e.g. a picture, a piece of writing, or a memorabilia. For instance, if I want to visualize myself as a good speaker, I might want to put on a video of the greatest speaker I know of. And then it will be much easier to create a mental image of me

speaking to an audience.

Practice: visualizing is not something you do just once and then forget about it. You have to do it consistently until you master calling up the images and memories. It becomes part of you, so real, that if it should happen you'll not be surprised.

Listen to your intuition: you might want to listen to your intuitive side and take instructions. Visualizing is a very surreal pursuit that triggers inspiration as well. In the highly creative process of calling up an image, you might find a solution to your other unrelated problems. Don't let it pass. Just free yourself.

Focus on the positive side: focus on what you want to achieve instead of the negative aspects. For instance, if you want to meet someone and make a good impression, call up an image of you talking to that person while looking very confident instead of focusing on anything that might go wrong and embarrass you.

Employ all your senses: try to make your visualization as vivid as you can. Instead of just painting a mental image, you could imagine even sounds and colors and dialogs. The more vivid your imagination is the higher your creative drive.

Improve your moods: you'll find that it'll be a lot easier to visualize when you are in a great mood than when you are feeling lousy. The quickest way to boost your mood is to consume some entertaining media. Also, you can improve your moods through increasing awareness and knowledge.

Think about what to do: your goal is to shift what you see in your mind's eye into reality. So you should develop a plan that will actualize your goal. For instance, if you want to become a star during a social event, creating a mental picture alone won't help, because you have to back it up with actions. So, develop a plan that will be useful in attaining your goals. If you are creative enough, you should know the necessary steps to take.

Don't be a dreamer: don't live in your head so much that you forget to live your actual life. Always be aware that you could lose yourself in the dream-world and miss life. In order to prevent this from happening, you should come up with a schedule that divides up your time over your interests.

Create a vision board: these are materials that will keep reminding you of your goals. A vision board is a collection of objects that represent your goals. You should put the vision board at an easy-to-see place so that it acts as your constant reminder of your important goals.

Seek results: you have written your goals, you have utilized your powers of visualizing, but now what's left is to make that goal real. So, you should look for real-life situations in which you expect your goal to play out. If you have been meaning to improve your social skills, now go out and meet people and soon you will see a replication of what you had visualized.

Creating a vision board is a big part of visualizing. A vision board will feature images, affirmations, and other relevant objects. A vision board, also called a dream board or a treasure map serves the purpose of reminding you constantly of your big goals and dreams.

Key things to remember before creating a vision board:

Decide why you want to be good at socializing: maybe you want to develop social skill in order to be good at communicating your ideas, or maybe you are just tired of being a wall flower and want to shine for the first time in your life, or maybe you want to be popular for the sake of being popular. Whatever your reasons for wanting to have social skills, just note them down.

Create your theme: what is the focus of your vision board? You should create a vision board that is aligned to one overriding goal. If you want to become great at socializing, the vision board should display objects that boost a person's ability to socialize. It could be collages of happy-go-lucky people having a conversation. You want to use the best photos and images. Also, there should be descriptive words to capture the spirit of the photo and call back your hunger for your goal.

Place your vision board where you'll see it every day: your vision board carries your hopes and goals, and so there's no need to hide it in a closet, you should instead put it in an open position where you'll see it on a day-to-day basis. However, if you want to give people no clues, you may hide it in a private place that only you can see, e.g. your bedroom.

Recognize a vision board for what it is; don't buy into the delusion that a vision board is all that you ever needed to succeed. The key role of a vision board is to remind you of your important life goals. However, if you are to succeed, you will need to go out there and take action. A vision board should not be only used as a reminder of important goals but also as a convenient organizational tool.

Chapter 9

SOCIAL ANXIETY DISORDER AND CULTURAL DIFFERENCES

Cultural differences have been associated with mental illness and with social anxiety disorder, it can vary depending on the area that a person currently resides in and culturally how they were raised. Different cultures have different behavioral rules and regulations, especially for genders. What may be socially accepted in the United States may not be for India, Japan or opposite. For example, in Indian cultures, they don't put their own needs and desires first out of fear of what others may think. In comparison to western cultures, people put their own happiness first, regardless of what others may think of their actions later on. Indian culture also focuses more on the traditional aspects of life, focusing on society and how society views the individual as well as their family.

Calculations result that anxiety disorders affect approximately 10% of the global population. These are physical traits that tend to be chronic, consistent, and associated with a systematic cause of disability. In 2010, this medical condition caused a group of 30 European Union countries $84,184 to help individuals suffering from social anxiety alone.

As of May 2019, the National Comorbidity survey showed that there are different rates of social anxiety disorder within different cultural groups. Overall, the survey shows that social anxiety disorder is found to be less common in countries located in Eastern Asia. The survey showed that Russia and South American countries prevalence for social anxiety disorder were closer in numbers to the United States compared to Korea, China, Japan and Taiwan. The survey analyzed over 40,000 people and found those individuals that are at a lower risk to have social anxiety disorder are males, Native American population, Asian population, Hispanic population, African American population and those individuals who live in urban areas.

Cultures vary depending on mental health diagnoses and psychiatrists as well as mental health clinicians who have pointed out that the culture's diagnosis process may also differ depending on the culture and ethnic background. Some cultures have specific type of mental disorders that are linked or very similar to social anxiety disorder.

For instance, Japan and Korea have a mental disorder which they refer to as *Taijin Kyofusho (TKS)*, which alludes to how a person worries about being publicly watched or personally offending other people. Individuals with TKS typically avoid a wide range of social engagements.

Comparing this to people who suffer from social anxiety disorder, their fear is more about embarrassing themselves, as opposed to TKS, which is the fear of embarrassing other people around them. Those with TKS are more concerned with the repercussions of their behaviors towards others, such as their parents. Individuals who live with TKS often have anxious feelings of giving off body odors, giving inappropriate facial expressions, looking or focusing improperly, as well as blushing and making eye contact. Men tend to be diagnosed more often with TKS than females and they typically only account or possess one mental disorder as opposed to other countries that have coupled mental disorder challenges (social anxiety disorder and depression). This is quite unusual compared to those living in the United States, but researchers state this is the result of cultural differences. Research has also found there aren't a lot of statistical differences between the treatments of mental disorders between cultures; however, American males who are diagnosed with SAD tend to take longer to seek treatment.

The way a person expresses their social anxiety disorder does depend on the culture that they live in. Countries that have a more personal or individual focus have different views and fears then those who focus on the society as a whole and everyone is one person who plays a part in it (collectivist).

Societies that focus on everyone as a whole have tendencies to be more understanding and open to individuals who have more withdrawn behaviors; which correlates with the data that confirms the lower rates of social anxiety disorder in Asian countries. Cultures that have a more individualist outlook cause those with social anxiety disorder will come to blame themselves for their disorder and behaviors anxiety and those cultures that have a more collectivist perception on the world will cause the individual who has social anxiety disorder to feel more shame for their disorder and behaviors. An interesting study conducted on social anxiety disorder and Chinese people concluded that they often have a fear of making other people uncomfortable as well as causing them to behave in ways that will not be beneficial towards them or society.

When individuals are being treated for social anxiety disorder, especially if they are not native to the United States, their cultural background should be taken into consideration when determining how they should be tested for a mental disorder. What may be considered appropriate in the United States may be viewed completely different in their native countries such as China or the Middle East.

The rate of this disorder occurring varies largely between countries. It has been estimated and studied that anxiety disorders affect 5.3% of African populations and 10.4% for European populations. Social anxiety disorder may develop very early, such as in age of 5 to 10 years, compared to panic disorder and generalized anxiety disorder, for instance. In addition, SAD develops earlier than post-traumatic stress disorder, which typically appears between the ages of 24 and 50.

In 2017 *WHO World Mental Health Survey Consortium, published their findings* in JAMA Psychiatry analyzing the findings that researchers concluded that wealthier countries have a population that has more anxiety disorders then poorer countries. The study found that higher income countries had a larger proportion of individuals in their population that suffered from generalized anxiety disorder which is defined as someone who has consistent and overwhelming worry to the point where it affects their life overall. For example, Australia and New Zealand both identified as being high-income countries with an overall number of 15.9% of people living with a generalized anxiety disorder, social anxiety included. Nigeria had the lowest reported rates of anxiety disorder with a 0.1% of the population. They were considered to be a low-income country.

Researchers have concluded that the possibility of the ubiquitous results between lower-income countries because of the respective political and economic instability of the country. These specific circumstances potentially could have been directly contributing to higher rates — or possibly indirectly resulted in lower rates of anxiety disorders, since people might not report "excessive or abnormal" anxiety because their worries were justified by the issues they are being faced with. Unfortunately, not much research has been done and actually reported giving this much data in so many different countries since the diagnostic criteria for generalized anxiety disorders since 2013. One other fact to note that is an apparent limitation to contrasting pervasive rates across countries is that cultural and social influences play a role in how likely the individual will self-report symptoms of anxiety to the researcher questioning them or that the researcher would consider to be scientifically or clinically significant to the results. Typically, generalized anxiety disorders have been defined in countries primarily like the United States as opposed to non-Western countries.

Chapter 10
CHALLENGING COGNITIVE DISTORTIONS AND NEGATIVE THOUGHTS

Cognitive distortions deal with a whole negative mindset which hinders the way of confidence development.

Every person holds some automatic thoughts and the cognitive distortions then this mindset will be full of unhelpful and faulty belief. These distortions need to be identified so that one can easily start the quick response against them. A list of some common cognitive distortions is described below:

To urge for Perfectionism

While setting the goals in the professional and personal lives we become very much idealistic and start thinking about getting the most ideal part. The same is the case with social interactions. Under the influence of perfectionism, you may start believing that you want the best in a social gathering or any other event. The belief on perfectionism urges people to behave exceptionally in a job interview, without considering that there will be many different things which will be held accountable for the success of the interview.

Do or Die Thinking

Most of the people who suffer from social interactions have a habit of seeing things in concrete black and white terms and want each and every performance to relate to this concrete continuum. For instance, if one has to deliver a presentation then under the cognitive distortions, one will not feel satisfied unless every single individual will talk about the success and effectiveness of the presentation. Again, the social anxiety is developed from these misconceptions that success is all about do or die condition. Start taking the things positive and avoid being too judgmental.

Focus on Mind Reading

The people who suffer from social anxiety think that all the people around them think negative about them. Although they may not have any clear evidence regarding this fact yet the base their assumptions on the notion that they can easily read other people's mind. As a result, their social anxiety keeps on getting more prominent and avoids people thinking that they are disliked by them. Have a belief that you are not too good at reading mind, if you have some problem in social connections, you can also have the problems in mind reading as well.

Discounting the Pessimism

When a person is suffering from social anxiety, it is usually accompanied with pessimism. Under the influence of these two affects the person starts getting gloomy. His personality is developed in a way which only focuses on the bad outcome. For example, rather than enjoying the memory of those several parties which you experienced in the past, the dilemma of social anxiety will focus only on the only those times which turned out awkward or uneasy for the person.

Looking for Flaws

When the person who is suffering from social anxiety starts thinking about a particular session of social conversation or gathering, then the only thing which comes in his mind is to start recapping the flaws in that particular session. Negativities and flaws usually overcome the positivism and achievements. It will have two effects; firstly, the person will keep on thinking about the negativities and will not get any tome for improving and polishing the skills which were present in that episode. Obviously, flaws are everywhere and no one can claim to be a perfect person but only focusing on your weaknesses is your biggest weakness and you need to have a piece of thorough knowledge about your. You will feel confident.

Generalization of a scenario

As compared to flaws which deal with the weaknesses of the personality, generalization deals with the weaknesses present in the scenario. Now if you are aimed at eradicating the social anxiety then there are many chances that you have to fight against the generalizations. Never consider that the whole situation was negative so the outcome will be negative. There are always hidden opportunities in every kind of situation.

Emotional Reasoning

If you have a firm belief that you are a loser and people see you as a loser you will start behaving, in the same way, if you believe that you are confident then all of your actions and behaviors will be directed in the same way. Emotional reasoning will divert you to think that what you feel emotionally — you are inclined to do like it. You can eventually come to a point where these kinds of emotional reasoning will convert into permanent behaviors. So the more positive emotional reasoning you attain, the greater will be the chances that you eventually come up with a more socially acceptable and strong personality.

Converting Predictions into Facts

Social anxiety always leads you to predict negative and behave negative, you start predicting negative and eventually all you get is negative. For example one of the major prediction which social anxiety claims that the person will not be successful in the gathering so the results are equal to the prediction.

Assuming that You Are the Centre

One of the major reasons for being in social distress is to consider one's self as the most critical figure in the gathering, as if everyone will be noticing you only. This overemphasis will lower down your confidence and enhance your shyness. Try to be a free bird in this universe who is accompanying many other birds and the one who will be looking at these birds will see them as a whole so having a feeling that all the focus will be one single bird is not practical to be understood.

The Theory of Relativity

Relativity is the major reason of so much distress. Apart from social anxiety many different social catastrophes also result due to relativism. People in a social gathering start comparing themselves with others and judge their own selves with a relative approach with others. It is done without considering the physical and environmental variables which are usually accounting the success of other people. Every person follows a different destiny and eventually he will meet this destiny, in one way or the other.

Social anxiety demands a confident and assured behavior so that one can leave permanent impressions in a social gathering.

Chapter 11
DIET AND EXERCISE

A regimen of a balanced diet and working out has a positive impact on self-esteem. Working out boosts the levels of the feel-good hormones, and a balanced diet optimizes your physiological functions, all of which go toward making you feel like royalty.

What are some of the other benefits that the combination of diet and exercise bestow on your life?

Improved concentration: exercising is a great way of clearing the mind. Also, having a great diet means that the brain gets a steady supply of nutrients and oxygen and it works at its optimum best.

Alleviate boredom: it's easy to fall into the routine of going to work and back home and over and over again. But when you start pursuing fitness goals, you distract yourself from your repetitive and boring life.

Reduced risk of diabetes: diabetes is likely to affect people who are sedentary. And so, working out regularly and having a great diet will see to it that your blood sugar is stable.

Stress remover: working out tends to alleviate the stress of day-to-day existence. Cardio exercises are especially effective at boosting moods.

Great figure: someone who takes exercising and diet seriously will stand out because of their great shape. If you have an above-average body, well, it may not automatically make you confident, but it will go a long way in boosting the image that you have of yourself.

Having a balanced diet and observing a great exercise regimen is not as easy as it sounds. There are many parts that need to fall into place. First, you need to figure out what foods to eat, the right portion size, and how to prepare these foods. Also, you need to tailor your fitness program to your needs.

Carbohydrates are responsible for fulfilling the most energy requirements of the body. Simple carbs like sugar tend to cause a spike in blood sugar and the body releases too much insulin, while complex carbs are digested at a much slower rate.

Differentiate good fats from bad fats. The kind of fats that you are supposed to consume on a regular basis includes mono-unsaturated fats and omega-3 fatty acids. However, trans-fats and saturated fats have a negative impact on the body.

Foods that fight cancer and heart health diseases should be your priority. In this age of lifestyle diseases, it is very easy to eat your way into a disease. Some of these foods include Salmon, Cranberries, Blueberries, Lentils, and Legumes.

Document what you have been eating: your intention is to incorporate a great diet into your lifestyle. So start by documenting all the kinds of foods you have been eating, and then figure out what needs to go. For instance, if you have been binge drinking alcohol at night, you need to reduce alcohol intake or do away with it.

Create a plan: this involves pooling your diet together. It's like creating a timetable but instead of a lesson, you have food instead. Ensure that you list down all your favorite healthy dishes.

Balanced diet: the best diet should feature vital minerals and vitamins. Having a balanced diet is critical to optimizing your physiological functions. A balanced diet features foods drawn from a variety of food groups. When you combine a balanced diet and varied diet you create a most nutritious diet that gives you all the vital vitamins and minerals.

Go big on vegetables: your momma was right about veggies. They are one of the most nutritious food groups. Vegetables and fruits are loaded with fiber, vitamins, and antioxidants. Vegetables like spinach and kale have very high nutritional value and should be eaten as often as possible.

Lean protein: protein provides the body's building blocks. Foods that are rich in lean proteins include eggs, beef, fish, and legumes.

Whole grains: foods such as bread and pasta originate from grains. Grains are loaded with a lot of vital minerals and vitamins. Whole grains are organic foods and they help in boosting the functioning of various organs of the body including, skin, brain and digestive systems.

Drink water: water is an understated component of a nutritious diet. A person should consume water regularly throughout the day for maximum health benefits.

Be creative: where food is concerned, there's a big room for creative expression. For instance, rather than snacking on unhealthy foods, you might want to buy cookbooks and get recipes for healthy snacks. Cookbooks not only allow you to make healthier alternatives of your favorite foods but they also broaden your ability to fix healthy meals.

Exercise also plays a great role in improving mental health. The effectiveness of a particular workout regimen varies for different people. But with the right mix of type and intensity, you stand to gain the most.

Select your exercises: there are different types of exercises, including; aerobic, strength, stretching and balance exercises. Each exercise is suited for a particular objective, but in order to achieve optimal health benefits, one might consider combining all of them.

Practice moderation: ideally, you should perform the exercises in moderation. The USDA recommends doing cardio at least every week. Cardio exercises have great benefits such as loss of weight, low risk of diabetes, better moods, and reduced blood pressure.

Resistance training: strength training or resistance training helps in building your muscle mass. It is best performed in the correct weight category else you risk injuring your body.

Wear the right gear: if you are a regular at the gym, it'd be prudent to wear the right attire, chiefly because you are going to use many complex machines that require great care. You are supposed to wear non-restricting clothes and training shoes.

Remember to hydrate: water plays a big role in the effectiveness of a workout. When your body is hydrated, you can flash out toxins and keep a good pH environment and also help in the muscle building process.

Warm-up: instead of walking to the gym and then straight away to the weights, you might want to do some warm up exercises first. Warm-up exercises are usually less intense exercises such as skipping ropes. A warm-up exercise relaxes your muscles and makes you ready for strenuous activity.

High intensity exercises: these include high-intensity exercises that are done sporadically. Anaerobic exercises build your body's ability to adapt to extremely strenuous moments. Anaerobic exercises are especially useful in losing weight and building stamina.

Run: running is everybody's favorite choice of exercise. The best thing about running is that it is free and can be done anywhere. But it helps if you invest in a pair of great running shoes. Running helps greatly in improving heart health, managing weight issues, and clearing the mind.

Develop your abs: many polls say that defined abdominals is about the most aesthetically pleasing group of muscles. So you might want to target these muscles and make them pop. When you develop your abs, you will have a great posture, and also you will be much more resistant to spinal injury.

Perform planks: you assume the position of doing a pushup, but instead of going down and up, you just contract your abs and hold yourself in place. It is a very exhausting exercise.

Crunches: this is another exercise great for developing your core muscles. You lie down facing up, knees folded, and arms crossed. Then you lift your head toward your folded knees; go back down, then up again and so on.

Chapter 12

NATURAL REMEDIES

Anxiety is a burden that lowers the quality of life of those whom it affects. People with this condition seek out various treatments. A certain breed of people would rather seek natural remedies against anxiety as opposed to medication.

<u>Herb and oil</u>: there are many herbal treatments available. The herbal treatments have little side effects and they have the advantage of being natural. However, special care should be taken when buying some of these herbs from supermarkets because there is a suspicion that some cartels sell contraband under generic herbal labels. Herbal treatments are not only useful for anxiety but also heart problems, bowel movement, and emotional instability.

<u>Catnip</u>: catnip is part of the mint family and is used in treating various anxiety-related symptoms such as stomach pain, headaches, and light-headedness.

Chamomile: this supplement is best used to treat mild anxiety. Chamomile is used to treat the symptoms of anxiety such as stomach pain and nervousness.

Fennel: this natural supplement is used in treating anxiety, constipation and indigestion.

Kava Kava: this supplement is used for treating moderate and severe anxiety.

Hops: the medical utility of hops is well documented. The supplement is effective for treating insomnia and headaches.

Motherwort: this supplement is for treating anxiety symptoms stemming from menstruation.

Passionflower: this supplement is great for alleviating mood swings and headaches.

Skullcap: this supplement not only alleviates anxiety symptoms but is also effective in treating inflammation.

St. John's Wort: this natural supplement is great for alleviating the symptoms of the major depressive disorder, including anxiety.

Valerian Root: this supplement is used in reducing muscle tension and stress.

Lavender oil: research shows that Lavender is great for alleviating muscle tension, uneasiness, and migraines.

GABA (Gamma aminobutyric acid): this amino acid reduces anxiety-related symptoms and eases muscle tension.

Ashwagandha: this herb helps in stabilizing moods and alleviating anxiety-related symptoms.

But before you start using herbals, some ground rules to keep in mind:

- Complement herbal treatment with a healthy lifestyle
- Ensure you have no allergic reactions
- Don't use herbs for long without medical advice
- Never take more than the appropriate dose
- *Don't mix herbal supplements with other chemical substances*

Clean diet

There's a direct link between the foods we eat and our mental health. Consuming too much food or too little of a particular kind has psychological implications. A poor diet consisting of sugars and trans-fats will cause a person to become overweight, and further than that, it'll likely trigger low self-esteem because of the poor image.

Armed with this knowledge, one should make a conscious effort of improving their nutrition. Foods rich in magnesium, vitamin B, calcium, and omega-3 fatty acids are known to reduce anxiety. Also, anti-inflammatory foods are great for both alleviating anxiety and elevating moods. These are some of the foods that one should add into their lifestyle:

- Fish
- Lean beef
- Chicken

- Eggs
- Nuts/seeds
- Dark green vegetables e.g. kale
- Fruits
- Legumes
- Whole grains

Eliminate sugar

Sugary foods lead to a spike in blood sugar, which causes the body to secrete too much insulin, and these conditions create an enabling environment for anxiety and depression. Sugary foods are known for causing unstable moods, inflammation and reducing overall brain health. Some of the foods laden with high sugar content include: cakes, biscuits, fizzy drinks, fast foods, and most other processed foods.

Reduce (or eliminate) alcohol intake

Some people battling anxiety may turn to alcohol under the false belief that it will suppress their anxiety. Well, it does suppress their anxiety, but only for a short time and then it necessitates more drinking for prolonged sustenance of the feeling. However, once their body catches up, usually after a hangover, depression comes back with a ten times intensity. So, if you're battling anxiety, the best action is to reduce alcohol intake or remove it altogether.

Improve your sleep

Having quality sleep has a great impact on your mental health. Studies show that the average person should sleep for six to eight hours every day in order to be productive. But the quality of sleep really matters. It is far better to sleep a lesser amount of hours in an enabling environment, than to sleep in a noisy environment for extended amounts of time.

Yoga and meditation

Yoga promotes the realignment of your body and most yogis' report elevated moods after performing yoga. Yoga also alleviates anxiety-related symptoms such as stomach cramps. Meditation is also a critical player in alleviating anxiety.

Improve your breathing

Practice taking deep breaths at the onset of anxiety. This has a calming effect on your mind. It will help stabilize your moods and have a clear mind.

Sunbathe

When you expose yourself to sunlight, your body creates vitamin-D, which is an essential vitamin in fighting symptoms of anxiety disorders and depression. Also, vitamin-D plays a critical role in boosting Serotonin – the hormone responsible for elevating feelings of happiness.

Epsom salts bath

Epsom salts lower blood pressure and alleviates anxiety symptoms. Also, the hot bath goes a long way in making you feel revitalized and thus you are more capable of battling any anxieties you may have.

Do what you enjoy

At the onset of anxiety, you might want to turn to another activity in order to ruin the train of negative thoughts. Immediately turn to an activity that brings you feelings of joy. This is a classic distraction. Well, refusing to face your problems might not work in the long term, but it is a great survival technique for the short term.

Go out

If anxiety attacks you while you're inside the house, you might want to step out. Being outdoors helps in reducing the symptoms of anxiety, particularly when you are engaged in some physical activity.

Entertainment

Whenever you experience fear or anxiety, you might want to turn on the music, this happens because of music as the ability to distract the mind. Also, you may engage in other forms of entertainment such as books and movies.

Laugh

Where's your sense of humor? Instead of being all gloomy, you should instead learn to see the humor in your flaws. So when you feel anxiety taking over you are free to poke fun at yourself. And considering that nowadays we have Twitter and Facebook, you might even post the joke online.

Face your fears

Ultimately, anxiety is a sign of an underlying problem. Be courageous enough and face your fears. In most cases, fear is imagined. You can only get over your fears once you live through them.

Research

It is said that what you don't know cannot harm you, but in this case knowledge is power. Try to research on the topic of anxiety and find out as much information as there is. You will be able to gain a clearer understanding of your situation and find avenues for seeking help.

So many people have elected to solve their anxiety using natural methods. Consistency in the treatments is critical, and above all increasing your knowledge.

Chapter 13

THE MEDICAL SIDE OF SOCIAL ANXIETY

Most people think that social anxiety is all in your head and that you can just cure it by trying to enjoy yourself while being out in public, but that is not the case. While it is all in your head, it is an actual medical condition that should be taken seriously. The hardest part to get people to understand is that there is currently no cure. Scientists are working on finding one, but there currently are only treatments to help ease the symptoms, not erase them entirely.

What Causes Social Anxiety?

No one really knows what the actual cause of social anxiety is. However, it is highly linked to other mental disorders, as well as trauma that has occurred in a person's life. If you have bipolar disorder, depression, PTSD, or insomnia you are more likely to suffer from social anxiety. That is because these disorders make it harder for your brain to communicate with itself properly, and this can often cause anxiety in many forms, most commonly in social situations.

If you have experienced trauma, you are more likely to suffer from social anxiety due to your fear of the trauma happening again. When it occurs in this form, it is generally described as social phobia, because it is based on a literal fear of the public. It is viewed as a self-preservation technique to help protect yourself from experiencing the same horrific event again. However, it makes life very stressful, because even going to the grocery store is an arduous task. Generally, people who have suffered a trauma of some sort have more severe social anxiety than those whose anxiety is caused by another disorder. This isn't always the case, but most of the time, it is.

While scientists and doctors do not quite know what causes social anxiety, they have narrowed it down to those two triggers. However, they also think that a person's genetics might play a part. That is because there are a lot of people who suffer a trauma or have other disorders that do not suffer from social anxiety. Scientists believe that when you are born, some of your genes mutate slightly which makes it a lot easier for you to develop social anxiety in your life.

These genetics do not guarantee that you will suffer this disorder however, as you would need a trigger to set it off. In most cases, people do not suffer anything bad enough to trigger their social anxiety. However, in a lot of other cases, there are events or disorders that trigger it almost with ease. It all depends on the person and how intense the mutation is. Scientists are working to figure out if everyone is born with the genetic coding for social anxiety, or if only certain people are. Once they figure that out, they will be closer to finding a cure.

Why Do More People Suffer Now?

It is true that in this day and age, it seems like there are a lot more people suffering from social anxiety than before. While that may be true, it does not mean that people did not suffer social anxiety in the past. These were the people that were labeled as recluses and hermits in the past; the neighbors that didn't talk to anyone and were considered weird. Social anxiety is not a new thing, it is just that technological (and medical) advances have made it easier to understand.

However, it does seem that even though technology makes it easier to understand and recognize, there are way more cases of social anxiety than there were fifty years ago. Psychologists can confirm that it is becoming a pandemic, which is what leads scientists to believe that everyone is coded with social anxiety cues.

It leads one to wonder what is triggering the sudden rise in cases, and there is one answer that makes sense: bullying. Bullying has always been a problem in people's lives. Whether it is over the color of their skin, their size, or the way they talk, everyone has been a victim of bullying at some point in their life, it seems. However, now it is so much easier to bully someone with no consequences. The internet makes it easier to make fun of someone behind a screen because you can remain anonymous. Being a victim of constant bullying whether it is in person or over the internet can trigger a person's social anxiety.

There are a lot of other reasons why it could be more prominent. It could be that people are not being forced to be social when they do not want to be, or it could be something else entirely, such as the violence we see on television, the news, and in video games. There are a lot of different possibilities, and scientists are working to narrow it down so that they can find what truly triggers the disorder.

Can Not Being Exposed to Social Situations Cause the Disorder?

In a sense, yes. However, not truly, because people can become more relaxed in social settings once they have been exposed to them. If as a child you were not allowed to go to social functions for some reason, and you were home-schooled, you could feel discomfort or nervousness in social situations. However, that does not mean that it would last forever, and chances are you would be just fine once you learned how to pick up on social cues.

So while some people who have never really had social interaction may develop social anxiety, it is not directly linked to a lack of interaction. Chances are there is another reason entirely that you become socially anxious or that you have been your entire life.

Symptoms of Social Anxiety

As stated above, there are a lot of symptoms, and some are specific to the person with the disorder; however, there are several blanket symptoms that can help you decide if you need to possibly go get diagnosed. If you do have a grouping of these symptoms, it is best to talk to your doctor about a diagnosis, but more on that will come later on in the book.

Event-Related Symptoms

- *Feeling nervous about an upcoming event*: Oftentimes, the anxiety starts before you are even in public. It presents as a feeling of dread when it comes to a social event. You may be thinking of ways to get out of it so that you don't have to attend. If you often feel nervous about social events, chances are it is a sign of social anxiety. However, if it is only big events where you have to perform or something of the like, then you may want to hold off on self-diagnosis. Don't rule it out entirely, though; if you have a dread for those sort of events coupled with other symptoms, you could still have this disorder.
- *Being really early to an event*: A lot of times, a person with social anxiety will show up early to an event they didn't even want to go to in the first place. This is especially true if it is for something that is important in their life, such as a job interview. People with social anxiety do not like to be stared at, so the thought of walking in late terrifies them. However, even though they may arrive an hour early to the location, they often don't walk in more than fifteen minutes early. They use the extra time to "psych themselves up" for what lies ahead.
- *Waiting for someone else to enter before entering an event*:

This is a common thing that people with social anxiety do. As much as they hate being the last person in an event, they also hate being the very first, because they fear being embarrassed for being the first one there, or the doors not being open. They wait for someone else to show up before trying to go in. If it is an interview, they often try not to go in earlier than ten to fifteen minutes early.

- *Waiting for someone else to do something to do the same thing*: Oftentimes when at an event, doing simple tasks such as throwing something away will frighten the person. They will wait until they see somebody else doing something to do the same thing. However, they will not get up immediately, they tend to wait for a bit, and then get up. If you find that doing simple tasks such as this frighten you in public, you may have social anxiety.
- *Follow one person around the whole time*: A socially anxious person will not be comfortable by themselves. They will not want to go to an event without someone who makes them feel comfortable, and they will spend majority of their time with that person. However, they try not to follow them too much for fear of annoying them.
- *Hiding in a corner, bathroom, or other secluded areas*: When not following a person that makes them comfortable, a socially anxious person will generally find an area that is not crowded or a corner. If neither is available, they will spend some time in the bathroom, but not too long because they don't want to cause a line. Sealing themselves away allows them to center themselves a bit

before they go back out and try to socialize. Oftentimes, a socially anxious person will find a "safe space" to escape to before they do anything else. They scope out this area the minute they enter the venue.

These are some symptoms that can occur during big social events or interviews for a job/other important parts of your life. If you find you have problems with doing these, then you may need to talk to your doctor and see what you can do to ease your symptoms.

General Society Symptoms

- *Getting nervous when there are a lot of people*: A lot of times a person with social anxiety will not feel comfortable if they have to go to a place where there are a lot of people. This can be a restaurant, a store, anywhere in public where people tend to gather. It can make doing even mundane tasks like the weekly grocery shopping difficult, and downright unpleasant.
- *Fear of going anywhere alone*: This is a common fear that people experience when they have social anxiety. They often feel like they are a target when they go somewhere alone, and do not want to be noticed. This can cause a person with social anxiety to avoid doing the task they need to do or cause them to have a panic attack after doing so.
- *Not wanting to ask an employee a question*: This is something a lot of people who have social anxiety have trouble doing. When it comes to asking an employee for

anything, such as where to find something or if they can get extra ketchup, the idea seems scary. Oftentimes, they will ask the person they are with to do these things. If you often have a fear of talking to strangers, even to ask them a simple question that is a good indication that you may have social anxiety.

- *Avoiding the spotlight*: This is another problem socially anxious people have. They may not want to take credit for something or come off as extremely humble, when in reality, they just want to avoid a big huzzah over the whole ordeal. They may feel uncomfortable receiving awards or throwing birthday parties for themselves. Surprise parties are often the worst and can make a person with social anxiety very uncomfortable.
- *Avoiding speaking to strangers*: People with social anxiety are often seen as rude because they do not like talking to strangers. The reality is that they are terrified of embarrassing themselves in front of a stranger, so they tend to avoid the situation all together.
- *Overanalyzing a situation*: Oftentimes, after a social event, a person with social anxiety will stay up late analyzing everything that they did that day. They often will nitpick at the little flaws they had and feel just generally horrible if they said something the slightest bit off. They also think about all the things that they should have said, and often beat themselves up for not saying them.
- *Expecting the worst/lowered expectations*: People with social anxiety often have meltdowns when they are let down, so to avoid those meltdowns, they lower their expectations. By not getting their hopes up, there is no

Social Anxiety

way that they can be anything other than pleasantly surprised at the outcome. If you find that you do this, then you may be suffering from social anxiety disorder.

These are all symptoms that a person with social anxiety may experience when they are out in the general public, or just living their day-to-day lives. These symptoms can cause a person to not want to do their basic daily tasks or to forego them completely.

Physical Symptoms

- _Sweating_: People with social anxiety may find that they sweat a lot for no reason. This is because when they get nervous, their body starts to heat up due to the quickening heart rate. This causes the skin to release sweat from the sweat glands, causing excessive sweating.
- _Flushing_: This also happens when a person gets nervous, for the same reason that sweating happens. The heart rate picks up and then the skin starts to get redder. This may make you look and feel like you are running a fever when in reality it is just nerves.
- _Tightness in chest_: Oftentimes, a person will begin to feel like their chest is tightening up, or they can't catch their breath. This can be the precursor of a panic attack, but it can also happen when you feel fine. It is your body's subconscious telling you that you need to relax and that you aren't comfortable. This can often feel like a heart

attack or a serious problem, and if it happens often, it should definitely get checked out.
- _Dizziness_: A lot of socially anxious people will feel dizzy if they are overwhelmed with a situation. This is due to the fact that the body feels out of balance due to the amount of stress it is under. When this happens it is best to sit in a quiet place for a little bit to recenter.

These are some of the physical symptoms that you may experience with social anxiety. These physical symptoms can really make you feel uncomfortable and can even cause health problems later on in life. If you suffer from these, you should definitely get checked out by a doctor.

Symptoms in social situations

- _Avoiding public restrooms_: This is something that a person with social anxiety will try to do at all costs. If they do have to use a public restroom, they will try to only urinate rather than defecate. They are afraid that someone will judge them for doing what normal humans do. If they do have to use the restroom, they will try to enter and leave when no one is in the restroom, so that no one can see them and judge them.
- _Lack of stranger interaction_: People who have a phobia of social situations will often have a hard time socializing with other people. They will try to avoid talking to strangers and may feel uncomfortable if a stranger talks to them. This may cause them to come off as rude when in reality they are just extremely uncomfortable.

- *Eating in public*: Oftentimes, people with social anxiety have problems eating in front of other people. They try to find a place to hide to eat. In high school, these people may sit at a table themselves or try to eat their lunch in the restroom. In life, they may avoid going to a restaurant or sit in the back corner when they have to go to one. They may take small bites and eat really slow to not appear gluttonous, as well as to not draw attention to themselves. Some people can't eat in public at all.
- *Conversation initiation*: Socially anxious people often have a hard time initiating a conversation because they are so scared to say the wrong thing. This may cause a person to not talk to someone that they potentially like, or to not really approach anyone at all. This can cause a lot of problems with making friends and trying to branch out from the normal scenarios that they may encounter.

Social anxiety disorder can cause a lot of problems with people doing day-to-day tasks, such as returning items to the store. They may have trouble entering a room where people are already seated, or may even have trouble going to school or going to work if they work in the public eye.

If you are suffering from social anxiety, you may find that your life is a lot harder than it seems it should be. You may find that your quality of life is diminished from the way other people describe their life. If this is the case, you may have social anxiety.

If you feel you have social anxiety, the best thing to do is to start looking into getting treated for your symptoms. This will make your life easier to handle and make it a lot easier for you to do the daily tasks that you have had problems with up until this point.

When You Should Consult a Doctor

Seeking help is extremely important. While most of the time social anxiety is not a big health risk, the problems it causes could be causing other health problems. It also could be caused by an underlying health problem which could have triggered your social anxiety. For these reasons, it is always important to seek help and figure out the best thing that you can do for treatment, whether it be something in terms of medication or a different thing entirely. You want to make sure that you are not going to have issues with your health because your health is important. You want to make sure that you are living a quality life, because living as a hermit can have negative effects on you.

You should consult your doctor if you feel that you have any of these symptoms. If you have multiple symptoms listed here, or feel you relate to all of them, you should definitely get checked out.

Who you should see

One of the hardest parts about this disorder is trying to seek help. This disorder is sorely under-diagnosed due to this. Most people feel that they do not have anything seriously wrong with them, and that there are much bigger problems in the world than what they have. However, social anxiety disorder is really a big problem and can prohibit you from living life to the fullest. So you should definitely seek help. The only question is: whom do you turn to?

Most people immediately turn to a psychiatrist for help, but the problem with that is that a psychiatrist is not trained to look for underlying health issues and will only be able to diagnose you strictly with social anxiety disorder. You also need a proper checkup to decide if you are not suffering from something else entirely.

Your best bet would be to talk to your normal doctor first. He or she can run some tests to see what all is wrong and make sure that you are getting the right diagnosis. They will make sure that you are not just getting a blanket diagnosis, and will help pinpoint exactly what it is that you need to get better.

It is important that you keep your appointment with your doctor and don't back out. You want to get healthy, and your doctor is there to help you. A good practitioner will listen to your worries and will not try to make you feel silly for having these feelings. It is best to remember that your doctor is a professional and knows about these things, and his only concern is to help you get better. He or she will not make fun of you.

What to expect

You will probably have to go through a series of visits to get your diagnosis. Unlike with the flu or strep throat, it takes time to diagnose someone with a mental illness. This is not something that is super easy to just write a prescription for, and since there is no cure, doctors tend to be very thorough before diagnosing a person with this mental disorder.

On the first visit, you will probably have to answer a bunch of questions about your day to day life and how you feel on a regular basis. It is important that you answer all of these questions - and that you answer them honestly. Your doctor is not going to call you out on anything, and laws prevent him from calling the cops for anything. You should tell your doctor if you are regularly consuming any illicit drugs, smoking, or abusing alcohol as well. This will help him pinpoint exactly what your problem may be, and if it is actually social anxiety or if your insecurities are caused by something else entirely.

The second visit, you will probably have to get some blood drawn for blood testing to make sure that your blood levels, iron and other things are normal. Having problems such as low iron can cause your brain to be stressed out, which in turn causes a social anxiety-like paranoia. Because of this, your doctor will want to make sure that your iron is where it is supposed to be.

You may also have to fill out some questionnaires and go in depth about how you are feeling. You will have to be completely honest with these questionnaires, so make sure that you are answering every question to the best of your ability. It is also good to make sure you have another person there to help you, because sometimes other people can see you better than you see yourself.

Criteria for SAD

There are certain things that your doctor looks for before diagnosing you with social anxiety disorder. These things may seem like they would be obvious, but pinpointing these things can often be harder than you would believe.

The first indicator of this disorder is having a fear of social gatherings. However, it can be all social gatherings, or just a certain type. This makes it difficult because you have to know if it is an actual fear or if it is just a discomfort. Just a discomfort usually just indicates that the person is naturally introverted. You have to really be afraid of these functions to the point it can affect your attendance to them in order to have it be a criteria for social anxiety disorder.

These situations can and most likely do invoke panic attacks or feelings of disorientation. The criterion for these being related to social anxiety is that they are unfounded or seemingly are unreasonable due to the calm atmosphere in which you have them. You have to make sure that if you do have a panic attack that you are not in a situation where one would be hurt, such as an instance where you are in physical danger.

These symptoms have to affect your day-to-day functions to the point where it affects your quality of life. If they do not, it is too hard to diagnose this disorder, and most doctors will tell you that it is just stress or generalized anxiety.

Generalized or Specific SAD

There are two types of social anxiety disorder. They are known as generalized and specific social anxiety and are pretty self-explanatory, but we will still go over each one. Some people feel that if they are not anxious in every social event then they are not socially anxious. However, that is not true.

The people who think that are thinking of generalized social anxiety, where any social setting has the chance to make a person uncomfortable. This is what most people think of when they think of generalized social anxiety. While it is a problem in itself, it overshadows specific social anxiety and causes thousands of people to go undiagnosed each year, because they "don't have it that bad". If you have generalized anxiety you should definitely get treatment – just remember not to belittle someone who doesn't have it "as bad".

Specific social anxiety is where only one type of social event causes a person severe anxiety. The most common is eating in public. Some people simply cannot eat in front of other people and it can cause them to really feel bad about themselves. You want to make sure that you are going to get checked out if you are anxious in any situation enough to have a panic attack or to just not want to attend period.

A doctor can pinpoint if you have specific or generalized anxiety. You want to make sure that you are getting the diagnosis that you need, so you can get the appropriate treatment for you.

AFTERWORD

Thank you for downloading this book.

I hope it was able to help you learn more about social anxiety and offer practical strategies through which you can start managing your social and personal life more confidently and efficiently. I have included several action plans, practical strategies, and proven techniques for overcoming social anxiety, which may finally help you accomplish all your goals of fighting the social anxiety monster.

The book is packed with plenty of perception-changing techniques, social interaction tips, confidence-building strategies and other valuable anti-social anxiety hacks that will put you on the highway of being a more socially well-adjusted individual.

The next step is to take action. A person who does not read is as good as a person who cannot read. Similarly, knowledge without action is pointless. One cannot challenge social anxiety

Afterword

only by reading about it and feeling great. You have to go out there and practice it consistently to make it work for you! You have to sweat it out and give it your all to become one among the social butterflies you've always envied.

Here's to a social anxiety-free life!

Made in the USA
Coppell, TX
04 October 2020